Romeo and Juliet remains
produced plays. H
that it is v
neverth produced a long-runn
comic and tragic elements. This stim

- a scene-by-scene theatrically focuse ...mentary
- an introduction to the differences between the two Quarto and the Folio texts of the play
- excerpts from Shakespeare's source and other contextual documents
- a study of key performances on stage and screen, including the musical adaptation *West Side Story* and Baz Luhrmann's film *William Shakespeare's Romeo + Juliet*
- an overview of the debate about the play's status as a tragedy.

Edward L. Rocklin is Professor of English at California State Polytechnic University, Pomona, California. His previous publications include *Performance Approaches to Teaching Shakespeare* (2005).

The Shakespeare Handbooks are student-friendly introductory guides which offer a new approach to understanding Shakespeare's plays in performance. The commentary at the heart of each volume explores the play's theatrical potential, providing an experience as close as possible to seeing it in the theatre. The Handbooks also offer contextual documents, a brief history of the text and its first performances, case studies of key productions, a wide sampling of critical opinion and guidance on further reading. Ideal for students and teachers of Literature and Theatre, as well as actors and directors, the overall aim is to help a reader reach an independent and well-informed view of each play by imagining how it might be performed on stage.

THE SHAKESPEARE HANDBOOKS

Series Editor: John Russell Brown

PUBLISHED

John Russell Brown	*Hamlet*
John Russell Brown	*King Lear*
John Russell Brown	*Macbeth*
David Carnegie	*Julius Caesar*
Paul Edmondson	*Twelfth Night*
Bridget Escolme	*Antony and Cleopatra*
Kevin Ewert	*Henry V*
Trevor R. Griffiths	*The Tempest*
Stuart Hampton-Reeves	*Measure for Measure*
Margaret Jane Kidnie	*The Taming of the Shrew*
Ros King	*The Winter's Tale*
James N. Loehlin	*Henry IV: Parts I and II*
Jeremy Lopez	*Richard II*
Christopher McCullough	*The Merchant of Venice*
Paul Prescott	*Richard III*
Lesley Wade Soule	*As You Like It*
Martin White	*A Midsummer Night's Dream*
Edward L. Rocklin	*Romeo and Juliet*

FORTHCOMING

Alison Findlay	*Much Ado About Nothing*
Stuart Hampton-Reeves	*Othello*

The Shakespeare Handbooks

Romeo and Juliet

Edward L. Rocklin

First published 2010 by
PALGRAVE MACMILLAN

Palgrave Macmillan in the UK is an imprint of Macmillan Publishers Limited,
registered in England, company number 785998, of Houndmills, Basingstoke,
Hampshire RG21 6XS.

Palgrave Macmillan in the US is a division of St Martin's Press LLC,
175 Fifth Avenue, New York, NY 10010.

Palgrave Macmillan is the global academic imprint of the above companies
and has companies and representatives throughout the world.

Palgrave® and Macmillan® are registered trademarks in the United States,
the United Kingdom, Europe and other countries.

ISBN-13: 978–1–4039–9504–9 hardback
ISBN-13: 978–1–4039–9505–6 paperback

This book is printed on paper suitable for recycling and made from fully
managed and sustained forest sources. Logging, pulping and manufacturing
processes are expected to conform to the environmental regulations of the
country of origin.

A catalogue record for this book is available from the British Library.

A catalog record for this book is available from the Library of Congress.

10   9   8   7   6   5   4   3   2   1
19 18 17 16 15 14 13 12 11 10

Printed in China

TO JOSEPH AND MARION STODDER

'Of love and joy, see, see the sovereign power'

Contents

General Editor's Preface

The Shakespeare Handbooks provide an innovative way of studying the plays in performance. The commentaries, which are their core feature, enable a reader to envisage the words of a text unfurling in performance, involving actions and meanings not readily perceived except in rehearsal or performance. The aim is to present the plays in the environment for which they were written and to offer an experience as close as possible to an audience's progressive experience of a production.

While each book has the same range of contents, their authors have been encouraged to shape them according to their own critical and scholarly understanding and their first-hand experience of theatre practice. The various chapters are designed to complement the commentaries: the cultural context of each play is presented together with quotations from original sources; the authority of its text or texts is considered with what is known of the earliest performances; key performances and productions of its subsequent stage history are both described and compared; an account is given of influential criticism of the play and the more significant is quoted extensively. The aim in all this has been to help readers to develop their own informed and imaginative view of a play in ways that supplement the provision of standard editions and are more user-friendly than detailed stage histories or collections of criticism from diverse sources.

Further volumes are in preparation so that, within a few years, the Shakespeare Handbooks will be available for all the plays that are frequently performed and studied.

John Russell Brown

Acknowledgements

First, I would like to thank John Russell Brown, who invited me to contribute to this series and who has guided my work in drafting and revising this volume with a clear sense of the animating purpose – to enable readers to explore the opportunities for co-creative engagement provided by the text of a Shakespeare play.

I have benefitted from the work of those who have written earlier volumes in this series. While all of them have helped me discover the possibilities in this emerging genre, the books by John Russell Brown, M.J. Kidnie, and Kevin Ewert have been particularly instructive.

As will be evident, I have also learned from a wide array of scholars, critics, actors, and reviewers. But, as my citations attest, the work of Jill Levenson, James Loehlin, and Katharine Wright has been essential to my exploration of the intricacies of this play in performance.

In addition, a number of other people have contributed to this volume. Alan Dessen has been sharing his knowledge and ideas with me since we first met on a ferry in Seattle and discussed *Titus Andronicus*; and he has offered his insights on the productions of *Romeo and Juliet* we have seen together. Steve Urkowitz shared some of his recent work on the two quartos of the play, and the precision of his analysis has sharpened my own perception of the contrasting designs embodied in these two texts. Larry Green of the University of Southern California and Betsy Walsh of the Folger Shakespeare Library provided copies of important texts. I also benefitted from a conversation with Ed Gero, whose performance of Friar Laurence was a memorable element in the 2005 Folger Shakespeare Theatre production discussed in Chapter 5.

In 39 years of teaching, I have explored the play with hundreds of students, but I especially want to thank the students in English 551 at Cal Poly Pomona who, in the winter term of 2009, spent ten weeks probing the play's language and potentials. Albie Miranda, in particular, offered crucial insights into the process by which we come to know a play through reading its text.

At Palgrave Macmillin, Sonya Barker and Felicity Noble have been patient and helpful in keeping the process of writing and publishing this book moving forward.

A long-term debt to Joe and Marion Stodder is registered by the dedication.

Finally, I want to thank Kate Massey, my colleague and wife, who has provided unfailing encouragement and insight during this project, and who does indeed 'teach the torches to burn bright'.

Edward L. Rocklin

1   *The Text and Early Performances*

Texts

Romeo and Juliet exists in three different texts: the first Quarto (Q1), published in 1597; the second Quarto (Q2), published in 1599; and the first Folio (F), published in 1623. It is, indeed, one of what is now called Shakespeare's multi-text plays, and as is true with all these plays the existence of two or more texts creates challenges for editors, performers, readers, and scholars – and, as will be suggested, opportunities for thinking about performance.

The First Quarto – quarto volumes were created by folding large sheets of paper twice, creating four leaves and eight pages – was published with a title page reading *An Excellent conceited Tragedie of Romeo and Juliet, As it hath been often (with great applause) plaid publiquely, by the right Honourable the L. of Hunsdon his Seruants.* It contains about 2300 lines, making it about 800 lines shorter than Q2. For the first two acts, the words largely parallel those in Q2, although the opening Chorus is 12 lines instead of the familiar 14 of Q2. Starting with scene 13, however, in which Romeo and Juliet meet at Friar Laurence's cell to be married, Q1 often diverges from Q2. While the action is basically the same, many speeches in Q2 have no comparable speeches in Q1, and other speeches appear in Q1 in much reduced form. Particularly striking is the fact that the role of Juliet is 40 per cent shorter (Irace, 1994, p. 185), with major cuts in her soliloquies.

The Second Quarto (1599), entitled *The Most Excellent and lamentable Tragedie, of Romeo and Juliet,* announces that it was *Newly corrected, augmented, and amended: As it hath bene sundry times publiquely acted, by the right Honourable the Lord Chamberlaine his Seruants.* Q2 is about 3100 lines long and provides the versions of Juliet's soliloquies familiar to us from page and stage. It provides the basic text for modern editions, although part of Q2 (generally considered to be from 1.2.55 to 1.3.37) is based on Q1.

The First Folio of Shakespeare's plays, published in 1623, was put together by John Hemmings and Henry Condell, who were sharers in the company that, when James I became its patron, changed its name from the Lord Chamberlain's to the King's Men. The Folio – a large volume made from sheets folded only once – was published in 1623, seven years after Shakespeare's death. Scholars agree that the text of *The Tragedie of Romeo and Ivliet* was based on the Third Quarto, perhaps with some editorial work by a member of Shakespeare's company. Thus because Q3 was based on Q2, the Folio text does not serve as the basis for modern editions, but it is consulted for specific word choices. The Folio prints neither version of the first Chorus.

Scholars have devoted intense effort to discovering the origin and authority of the two quarto texts, in part because a clear and simple account of their relative authority might offer rich interpretive rewards. If, for example, Q1 was simply a shorter version of Q2, we might read it as an early draft which Shakespeare expanded as he revised and improved the play, perhaps based on experience in performance, and we could then study the two texts to learn about Shakespeare's process of revision as well as how that revision illuminates the intentions registered in Q2. However, the differences between the two texts are of many different kinds, and during the past 150 years these differences – some of which resemble differences in other multi-text plays such as *The Merry Wives of Windsor, Henry V, Hamlet, Othello,* and *King Lear* – have prompted scholars to offer competing hypotheses about the origins and functions of the two quartos.

For much of the twentieth century, 'the modern orthodoxy' (Levenson and Gaines, 2000, p. x), which is still presented in many scholarly editions of the play, has been to explain what was believed to be the 'corrupt' nature of Q1 by a scenario in which several actors in the company reconstructed the play from memory and, perhaps, their own individual parts, and sold this text to a publisher who paid a printer to issue the play. This hypothesis has seemed to offer a way to explain the discrepancies between what were often spoken of as the earlier 'bad' and the later 'good' quarto: the problems in Q1 were assumed to follow from the fact that the reporters remembered their own parts clearly, recalled the speeches of characters on stage with them less clearly, and had difficulty in reconstructing dialogue spoken when none of them were on stage. In the case of *Romeo and Juliet*, scholars have proposed the reporters included combinations of Mercutio, Paris, and Romeo. Q2, by contrast, was seen as a good quarto because it was printed from some version of Shakespeare's manuscript – a position that is still generally accepted.

During the last 40 years, however, memorial reconstruction has been challenged by scholars who have sought to discredit the entire hypothesis (Levenson, 2000, pp. 118–20). They have pointed out that there is no concrete evidence of any actor or actors reconstructing a play in the manner described, nor evidence of any play being stolen from the company for which Shakespeare wrote (Werstine, 1990, p. 68). They have also noted that even if several actors reconstructed a playtext such as *Romeo and Juliet*, it would not necessarily have been profitable for a stationer to authorize and a printer to publish such a text, since playtexts generally did not sell well (Blayney, 1997, pp. 388, 412). In addition, they have pointed out problems and contradictions in the analysis offered by the memorial reconstructors. For example, it has been suggested the one reporter was the actor playing Romeo, yet it hardly seems credible that Richard Burbage would have participated in stealing property from the company in which he held a share. Kathleen Irace proposes Mercutio as one of the reporters in order to explain some features of the Q1 text (pp. 126–8), but this raises the question as to why that actor produced what Brian Gibbons – a proponent of memorial reconstruction – derides as a distorted version of his own dying words in Q1 (1980, pp. 6–7). Such problems – and there are many more than can be touched on here – have led Paul Werstine to argue that the first quarto of *Romeo and Juliet* does not meet the rigorous criteria W.W. Greg established when he argued that the actor playing the Host was the reporter of the First Quarto of *The Merry Wives of Windsor* (1999, pp. 326–7, 332).

As the critique of memorial reconstruction has gained traction, two other hypotheses have (re)emerged. One proposes that Q1 is an abridgment by Shakespeare, by someone else, or by the playwright working with members of his company, and was created for performance on the stage under conditions which demanded a shorter text, although we cannot specify what those conditions might have been. This hypothesis is presented by Jay Halio in his *Guide* to the play, where he proposes that those who created Q1 sought to maintain the powerful plot while sacrificing some of the poetic dialogue, producing 'a swifter paced drama that loses little of its *dramatic* impact, whatever losses it may sustain in its poetry' (1998, p. 3). However, cutting the text in order to emphasize the plot does not explain some of the major differences between the texts, nor does it explain why the language of the last three acts deviates substantially from Q2. If the aim was to reduce long poetic passages, this might explain why some of Juliet's soliloquies were reduced, but it fails to explain why some of Romeo's long speeches were not, nor does it explain why Mercutio's Queen Mab speech, which seems even less necessary for the plot, remained intact.

The second hypothesis, proposed by Alexander Pope in his edition of Shakespeare's plays (1723–5), suggests that Q2 represents Shakespeare's revision of the draft published as Q1. This hypothesis also encounters problems, including the radical differences in the marriage scene. The contrast is summed up by Lukas Erne who writes that 'Although this scene dramatises the same event as the corresponding one in Q2, the text is almost completely different, as is its tone' (2007, p. 97). Moreover, scholars disagree about the merits of the two scenes: some, like Halio, find the Q1 version obviously inferior, while others, like E.A.J. Honigmann, note that 'many critics think it as good as, or better than, the definitely Shakespearian text' (1965, p. 134).

Finally, even as they argue over the relative quality of the two texts, most scholars have ignored how the scenes differ as blueprints for performance. These differences have been extensively analyzed by Steven Urkowitz (1988, 2008), who delineates the different performance options offered by each text. His work demonstrates that we can use the two texts to stimulate actors and readers to imagine varied realizations of the scenes.

At this point, the editorial argument about the quarto texts of *Romeo and Juliet* seems to have reached an impasse, since no single theory explains all the differences between Q1 and Q2, and each theory is open to fundamental challenges. Fortunately, we do not need to decide between these hypotheses. Rather, we can take advantage of the work of Jill Levenson who, in her Oxford edition, provides modernized versions of both quartos and argues that it is more accurate historically and more productive theatrically to regard them as two exemplars of the play. Read in this way, we can sharpen our perception of each text's unique elements and stimulate our imagination of how each may be performed. The Commentary works with the text of Q2 produced by Levenson. For other Shakespeare plays I will cite *The Riverside Shakespeare* (1997).

Early performances

While both quartos advertise a play that was publicly acted 'with great applause' (Q1), no record of performance has survived from the years before the Restoration of Charles II in 1660. Yet its popularity is suggested by the fact that, as G. Blakemore Evans notes, 'From 1598 to 1642, allusions to (or lines and passages imitated from) *Rom.* are outnumbered only by those to *Ham.*, *Venus and Adonis* and *1H4*' (2003, p. 1). Any discussion of what audiences in the mid-to-late 1590s witnessed and how they responded must be highly speculative, but it seems probable that three elements must have shaped the play's performance and reception: the roles of the two lovers; the sequence of scenes embodying the forces of love and hate; and the use of key features of the stage to create what became some of the most famous scenes in English drama. These elements continue to make the play successful, even when it is performed on stages quite different from those for which Shakespeare wrote and in mediums such as film and television whose potentials he could not have foreseen.

'Juliet and her Romeo' Simply witnessing a performance will demonstrate that the roles of the young lovers were intended to dominate the action, but Marvin Spevack's *Concordance* adds detail to that experience. By Spevack's count, Q2 includes eight roles of more than 100 lines: Romeo (616), Juliet (541), Lawrence (350), Nurse (280), Capulet (267), Mercutio (262), Benvolio (160), and Lady Capulet (114). Romeo's 616 lines are 19.8 per cent and Juliet's 541 lines are 17.4 per cent of the play, and the fact that together their lines constitute the same percentage of their play as Hamlet's lines constitute of his play suggests that we should see the lovers as a joint protagonist:

> Certainly the evidence of recent productions confirms the view that Romeo and Juliet must be thought of as a pair, to be cast together rather than as distinct individuals. The time the characters spend together on stage is so limited that the audience must instantly be convinced of their all-consuming love; otherwise the production must become unbalanced.
> (Holding, 1992, p. 75)

It seems likely that the first actor to perform Shakespeare's Romeo was Richard Burbage, the star of Lord Chamberlain's Men from their formation in 1594 to his death in 1619. If the play was first performed in 1595 or 1596, Burbage would have been 26 or 27 – younger than many famous actors who played Romeo until the second half of the twentieth century. Burbage would already have created comic and tragic protagonists in a number of Shakespeare's plays – good preparation for creating a figure who at first seems to be the protagonist of a romantic comedy before his own choices help enmesh him in a tragic action.

While the largest part belongs to Romeo, it is only the twenty-first longest role in the canon, and the eighteenth longest male role. Juliet, on the other hand, is not only the second largest role in the play but the fifth largest female role in the canon, surpassed only by Rosalind (721 lines), Cleopatra (670 lines), Portia (578 lines), and Imogen (591 lines). If *The Merchant of Venice* was composed after *Romeo and Juliet*, Juliet was the longest female role Shakespeare had yet written in a single play, and a major opportunity for a boy actor. The role clearly demands verbal dexterity and emotional power as it moves beyond the range of Shakespeare's earlier comic heroines in Juliet's love scenes, soliloquies, and suicide. If we include her first speech in 2.1 and her final speech in the tomb, Juliet's six soliloquies (in 2.1, 2.4, 3.2, 3.5, 4.3, and 5.3) total 127 lines or just under one quarter of the role; and during the fourth act Juliet must hold the stage without the banished Romeo. Indeed the plot emphasizes Juliet's autonomy as she makes a series of choices in which she encourages Romeo's wooing, proposes marriage to Romeo, consummates that marriage, rejects marriage to Paris, compels the Friar to develop a plan to save her from that second marriage, takes the potion which produces her apparent death and entombment, rejects the Friar's final plan to have her retire to a nunnery after Romeo's suicide, and kills herself in order to be reunited with Romeo. Juliet is at least as much an agent in shaping the lovers' fate as is Romeo.

'Here's much to do with hate' The love-scenes include Juliet and Romeo's initial encounter at the Capulet's feast (1.4); the window or balcony scene, where Juliet proposes marriage (2.1); Juliet's soliloquies (2.4 and 3.2); the scene before their wedding (2.5); their leave-taking, at the end of which Romeo descends from the window (3.5); her soliloquy before drinking the sleeping-potion (4.3); and their reunion in the Capulet tomb (5.3), where love and hate converge as Romeo kills Paris and each lover commits suicide as the only means to control their destiny. Poised against the love scenes are the scenes in which hatred produces violence, most prominently at the beginning, middle, and end of the play (1.1, 3.1, and, 5.3), and where each violent outbreak prompts the intervention of the Prince. The fight scenes in English Renaissance drama were powerful attractions because some portion of the men in the audience would have been trained in the code of honor and the art of defense. The pivotal mid-day fight would have resonated with many spectators as an example of what could happen on the streets of London, and Shakespeare and some spectators might have known of the encounter in which Christopher Marlowe was challenged by William Bradley and witnessed his fellow poet Thomas Watson kill Bradley in what the coroner determined was an act of self-defense (see Sources).

Balcony, bed, and tomb *Romeo and Juliet* would also have engaged the original spectators because, as Andrew Gurr has noted, this play, like *Titus Andronicus*, made exciting use of the resources of the stage: 'The more substantial features needed as part of the stage design and furniture are the balcony or "window" in 2.1 and 3.5, Q1's "bed within the Curtaine" for 4.3 and 4.4, and the monument in 5.3' (1996, pp. 21–2).

The two window scenes One of the most famous scenes in Shakespeare's plays, the so-called balcony scene was almost certainly performed with Juliet placed in the area above the stage that is better thought of as representing the window of her bedroom, while Romeo, on the main stage, was imagined as situated in the garden of the Capulet mansion. For the second of these scenes, which ends their only night together as a married couple, Q1 directs '*Enter Romeo and Juliet at the window*' (G3^r) while Q2 offers '*Enter* Romeo *and* Juliet *aloft*' (H2^v): so both texts direct that the scene begin at the window occupied by Juliet when they arranged their marriage. Q2 adds '*Enter Madame and Nurse*' (H3^r) but given that the scene would be radically different if Lady Capulet discovered her daughter in bed with Romeo, and that there is an '*Enter Mother*' on the next page, it seems clear that only the Nurse enters, warns the lovers, and then departs. Q1's '*He goeth downe*' (G3^v), indicates Romeo climbed down by the rope ladder. After his exit, Q1's '*She goeth downe from the window*' (G3^v) suggests Juliet descended the stairs in the tiring house, entered by one of the doors, and met her mother on the platform, bringing her bedroom with her.

Q1 '*She falls upon her bed, within the curtains*' 'Scholars have suggested three possible original stagings: a curtained bed introduced when the scene begins; a bed situated behind curtains in the discovery space; or a curtained structure projecting from the tiring-house wall. They have also considered the visual foreshadowing that would result if the tomb of 5.3 were located in the space occupied by the bed in this scene and 4.4' (Levenson, 2000, pp. 315–6). The Q1 direction suggests that Juliet fell on the bed after completing her soliloquy and drinking the potion. The bed with Juliet's body could have remained in full view through the discovery and mourning by the Capulets. Once Capulet ordered the Nurse to wake Juliet, she would simply have moved toward the bed.

5.3 The Capulet Tomb The stage directions give only the barest hints about how the Lord Chamberlain's Men staged the final scene. In response to the Q1 direction '*Romeo opens the tombe*' (K^r) Alan Dessen has written 'I may understand *Romeo*, but, after much effort, I still have considerable difficulty with both *opens* and *the tomb*' (1995, p. 176). In addition to Dessen, Richard Hosley (1959), Andrew Gurr (1996), and Leslie Thomson (1995) have demonstrated why the surviving evidence makes it difficult to determine what might have happened during the staging of the play's climax. One way to state the problem is to say that we have too little physical evidence and too much verbal evidence, so that the problem is partly created by the varied terms used by the *dramatis personae*: 'through the finale, it is called a "Vault" or a "grave" seventeen times, against six when it is called a "monument" or "Sepulchre", and six when it is the more neutral "tomb" ' (Gurr, p. 24). The combination of these words and the tools brought by Romeo and the Friar can be analyzed in a number of ways. Vault, sepulchre, and monument suggest an above-ground structure, and a crowbar would be a useful implement to force open its doors. A vault could be created using the central opening in the tiring house wall, perhaps with a structure inside with several bodies on display, as suggested in the illustrations by Walter Hodges for the New Cambridge edition of the play. A monument might be a structure pushed onto the stage from the central doors, as may have been done with Juliet's bed. A grave suggests underground burial, and Romeo's mattock and Friar Laurence's spade would seem appropriate to mime digging as they opened the trap door. However, as Dessen has established by analyzing 30 monument scenes in plays from this period, whatever language is used in the dialogue may refer not to a physical structure but to a fiction created by the dialogue, the props, the actors, and the imagination of spectators. That is, the dialogue may be so precise either because the dramatist wants to underline the action that *is* happening on stage or because he wants to compensate for something that is *not* happening but must be imagined. Finally, it may have been the case that in different venues the Lord Chamberlain's Men employed different stagings.

Exeunt omnes: 'tragedy's chronic problem of removing the bodies' In the theater the ending of a tragedy raises the question of how to stage the 'Exeunt omnes':

> The general rule, firmly identified by Michael Neill, that tragedies commonly closed with a funeral procession that took the corpses offstage, cannot be applied in this play. Such an ending would not serve the closure of *Romeo and Juliet*. You do not take corpses away when the scene is already set in a graveyard. Interring them afresh in existing graves, whether to be covered by the trapdoor or closed off by a curtain, was a simple solution to tragedy's chronic problem of removing the bodies. If all the bodies were expected to be lying inside the trap already, clearing the stage would have been exceptionally easy.
>
> (Gurr, p. 25)

The dialogue at the end of *Romeo and Juliet* provides no indication as to how the bodies of Paris, Romeo, Juliet, and, perhaps, Tybalt, were dealt with, not even offering something as simple as Fortinbras' order that Hamlet be carried off by four soldiers or the indication that a dead march be played at the end of *King Lear*. Modern productions develop their own solutions to if or how to get the corpses off stage and how to stage the exit.

Finally, it is also worth repeating that the women's parts were played by boy actors, so that in Shakespeare's time the erotic energies of the play were embodied not in the sort of explicit sexuality that is possible in present day theater but in the language spoken by the lovers. It is that language which first made Romeo and Juliet such compelling embodiments of romantic passion and commitment.

2 Commentary

Reading the script of a play

When we become immersed in a production of *Romeo and Juliet*, we have an experience which Michael Goldman has captured in a passage in which he reminds us that

> Everything in *Romeo and Juliet* is intense, impatient, threatening, explosive. We are caught up in speed, heat, desire, riots, running, jumping, rapid-fire puns, dirty jokes, extravagance, compressed and urgent passion, the pressure of secrets, fire, blood, death. Visually, the play remains memorable for a number of repeated images – street brawls, swords flashing to the hand, torches rushing on and off, crowds rapidly gathering. ... The dominant bodily feelings we get as an audience are oppressive heat, sexual desire, a frequent whiz-bang exhilarating kinesthesia of speed and clash, and above all a feeling of the keeping-down and separation of highly-charged bodies, whose pressure toward release and whose sudden discharge determine the rhythm of the play.   (1972, p. 33)

When we turn from watching such a performance to reading or re-reading a text of *Romeo and Juliet*, we will realize just how much the co-creative efforts of the director, designers, fight choreographers, and, most of all, actors – as well as the presence of our fellow spectators – have contributed to our experience. Reading the text, we will encounter the rich, varied language that we have heard in performance (and, almost certainly, speeches that we did not hear because they were cut from the production), but we will be conscious of how much is missing compared to the performance. We will encounter about 120 stage directions, but almost all of these directions simply specify entrances and exits. We will also realize that there are a number of implicit stage directions, as when Tybalt challenges Benvolio by saying 'What, art thou drawn among these heartless hinds?' (1.1.62).

But most of all we will be or will become conscious of the massive array of moment-by-moment choices – such as whether Mercutio reveals, tries to conceal, or is himself unaware of how seriously he has been wounded by Tybalt's rapier – that were made in creating the production which engaged us. We may also realize that, without becoming actors or directors or designers ourselves, it is possible to develop the ability to read the text of the play differently, finding both the mandated and the open elements and imagining alternative performances. 'Reading for performance', as M.J. Kidnie has written in a volume in this series, 'transfers the creative activity to readers who, unlike theatre practitioners who are required at some point to settle on particular choices, have the freedom to consider, and reconsider, multiple theatrical options and their interpretive implications' (2006, p. 142). The purpose of this Commentary is to assist those who want to develop their co-creative faculties as readers of drama so that they can become more fully engaged in imagining the performance potentials of this extraordinary play.

ACT I

Sunday morning to Sunday midnight

The Chorus: Framing options

During his career, Shakespeare experimented with a variety of ways to begin a play so as to initiate the action and situate the audience in relation to that action while also providing any necessary exposition. One device he employed was a double beginning, in which the first beginning framed and the second initiated the action. He did this in *The Taming of the Shrew*, with its induction and shrew-play, but apparently abandoned the framing story after the first act. And he did this in *Henry V*, using a Chorus who asks the spectators to participate in creating the play, who reappears before each of the next four acts, and who closes the play with an epilogue. In the Q1 and Q2 texts *Romeo and Juliet*, the play begins as if it might employ the pattern the dramatist later developed in *Henry V*, opening with a Chorus who also appears before the second act – but the Chorus does not return after this second speech. So this play presents what seems to be an incomplete frame: some productions keep both speeches, some use only the first, and some omit both.

But if the production begins with the Chorus, then what we usually see is a single actor walk onto the stage, survey us, and begin to address us. How is he dressed? In a costume from a particular period? Or from our own time? Does his costume foreshadow the setting of the play or contrast with it? What tone does he adopt? Does he point to locations for the two houses or look up at the heavens – as he might have done if the play was revived at the Globe, pointing to the heavens painted on the underside of the roof over the stage? Does he speak confidently, sure we will pay attention? Or is he pleading, as if uncertain of our engagement? How does he conclude his speech? With a bow toward us? With an arm pointing to the entering servants?

1–8 'Two households both alike in dignity'   In the first part of his speech – eight lines which compose the first two quatrains of what proves to be a sonnet – the Chorus provides us with a compact exposition, introducing the setting, the two houses, and the love between the children whose marriage ends in death and whose death ends the feud. In relinquishing the suspense which is usually such a powerful tool for securing our engagement, the prologue invites us to concentrate less on *what* happens and more on *how* it happens. The description of the lovers as 'star-cross'd' offers the first of a number of concepts through which we might interpret the action.

9–14 'Which but their children's end naught could remove'
The sestet which completes the sonnet does not provide the same density of information as the first eight lines, but rather stresses the causal relation between the children's death and the end of the feud. The rhymes alert us to the fact that this speech is in verse, and would have enabled some of the literate members of Shakespeare's audience to recognize that the speech is a sonnet, and thus to realize the play is being introduced by a form largely devoted to representing the vicissitudes of erotic and spiritual love.

Who delivers the Chorus? If, for example, the Chorus is performed by the Prince or Friar Laurence, this will inflect its significance. In the first case, the actor will highlight the impotence of the Prince to prevent the tragedy. In the second, the Friar will underline the irony that he manages to end the feud but only at the cost of destroying the

people he is trying to save. In this performance, as Bernice Kliman and
Laurie Magnus suggest, we may hear the Friar as 'exonerating himself' before the fact by presenting the tragedy as caused by fate (p. 2).
It is also possible to have the Chorus delivered by the whole cast (as
in P.J. Paparelli's 2005 production, discussed in Key Performances).
Or the Chorus can be spoken by a woman, or even all four women,
which might draw attention to the way this patriarchal society gener-
ates the forces that thwart the lovers, and prompt us to resist rather
than simply accept the imperatives of that culture. In Michael Boyd's
2000 RSC production, the Chorus was delivered posthumously by
Romeo during the opening riot, while the fighters were frozen in
place, and he could even address specific lines (ll. 10–11) to his father
(Tennant, 2003, p. 121). This maneuver was capped at the end of the
performance, when the lovers rose from the tomb and exited through
the audience as if moving toward an afterlife (Dessen, 2001, pp. 5–7).
Directors who omit the Chorus leave the audience members freer to
employ their own interpretive frameworks.

Act 1, scene 1: Day 1, Sunday morning

One of Shakespeare's resources for creating our experience and shaping our interpretation of that experience is his control of the flow of
bodies both within and between scenes, and the opening of this play
exemplifies this fact about the relation of text to performance. The
scene starts with two characters from the house of Capulet, increases
to four, then six as it bursts into violence, escalates rapidly to (say) 20
people with the entrance of the Prince and his train, before the violence is quelled and the stage empties, concluding with an encounter
between two characters, this time from the house of Montague. Thus
an essential element of our experience is that Verona is introduced
as a place where tensions run so high that, on what we later learn is
a Sunday morning (3.4.17–20), a person walking through the streets
may suddenly find himself caught in a potentially lethal brawl. How
serious is this brawl? The fighting may be staged so that, Tybalt aside,
the participants seem engaged in a ritual with no real intent to harm
one another. Or the brawl may provoke real violence, with some participants seriously or even mortally wounded. A comic brawl makes
the tragic encounter in 3.1 a shocking swerve from what might have
been a romantic play where the young lovers outwit their intransigent

parents to achieve a happy ending. On the other hand, a brawl that inflicts serious injuries shows that the tragic outcome is imminent from the start, and makes the fights in 3.1 seem almost inevitable.

1–53 'when I have fought with the men, I will be civil with the maids'   Two servants enter, speaking prose, and bring the feud to life. They are servants of the house of Capulet, they are armed with swords and bucklers, and they are eager to provoke a quarrel with counterparts from the house of Montague (ll. 1–7). They also establish two essential elements of the feud. First, they display a devotion to and delight in word-play that will characterize the younger generation, and their weapon of choice is the pun, especially the sexual pun: 'Draw thy tool' (30) says Gregory, to which Sampson responds 'My naked weapon is out' (32). Second, they present the paradigm which guides young males of the two houses in the passage from boy to man (ll. 20–2): you become a man by fighting with men from the other house and by having sex with the women of that house.

Two more servants enter, and may well have some difference in dress or ornament to signal their allegiance to the house of Montague. Their exchanges show that, while they are eager to fight, each pair wants to maneuver the other to make the first move so they can take 'the law of our side' (l. 44). Thus Sampson, who has been boasting of his martial and sexual prowess, is reduced to saying 'I do not bite my thumb at you, sir, but I bite my thumb, sir' (ll. 46–7) – using the equivalent to our gesture of giving someone the finger. They also parody the hair-splitting distinctions in the manuals of honor as they address each other as 'sir' 12 times in 16 lines, and the actors can vary their tones to emphasize the ironic potential in this term of ostensible respect. How brave are the four men? Gregory's remarks suggest Sampson is all talk and no sword (ll. 32–5). Is this the banter of male camaraderie or is Gregory registering how risky it is to start a quarrel with a coward as his partner? His decision to start the fight when Tybalt enters (ll. 54–5) can demonstrate the brutal calculation in 'honorable' violence: he starts the fight only when he thinks they will be joined by someone whose superior skill will tip the balance beyond the simple arithmetic of three against two, and he may suddenly be dismayed when it looks as if Benvolio, whose entrance he apparently misses, might make the odds even again.

54–68 'What, drawn and talk of peace? . . . Have at thee, coward'
Does Tybalt enter when Benvolio appears but refuse to intervene
because it is beneath his honor to fight with servants? Such a staging
will create a contrast with a Benvolio, who immediately intervenes to
keep the peace. Given Tybalt's first words, Benvolio must already have
drawn his weapon, providing a pretext for Tybalt to act as if he, too,
has the law on his side. Line 68 may be a necessary speech if Benvolio refuses Tybalt's challenge, serving as the insult which impels him
to fight – a pattern which may be repeated when Tybalt tries to force
Romeo to fight (3.1.66). Or Benvolio may be inhibited from fighting
because he knows Tybalt is a much more skilful swordsman.

69–70 'Clubs, bills, partisans! Strike, beat them down!' Jill
Levenson (2000, p. 148) points out that the Q2 speech heading, which
some editors present as Citizens, is actually '*Offi.*' and proposes 'Officer', which might signal a more effective group than 'Citizens', and a
group which might come close to subduing the six fighters. On the
other hand, 'Clubs' was the cry for apprentices to turn out, and those
who enter may actually contribute to turning the fight into a more
widespread brawl.

**71–6 'Old Montague is come,/And flourishes his blade in spite
of me'** Capulet enters, still not dressed for the day, calls for his 'long
sword' (l. 71), and proclaims he is ready to fight 'old Montague' (l. 73),
who has also entered. How old are the leaders of the two houses? In
Capulet's later conversation, his cousin insists it is 30 years since they
were last 'in a mask' (1.4.143), so it would seem that Capulet must be at
least 50 and perhaps 60 years old. The decision about how old Capulet
and Montague are shapes whether and how they fight. Do they engage
in serious combat? Are they putting on a public show to encourage
their followers? Or are they so feeble that they cannot lift, let alone
wield, the two-handed swords Capulet calls for? Perhaps things get
out of control because the two men bring on more armed retainers
who turn the fight into a riot.

The brawlers are armed with a variety of weapons and in the 1590s
the weapons would have served as markers of class, office, and exper-
tise. Sword-and-buckler was an old fashioned pairing and would have
been wielded with big 'washing' or swashing strokes (l.59). The long

sword was a weapon whose length and weight demanded a two-handed grip that made it hard to use, and it, too, would have seemed old-fashioned. Clubs were often used by apprentices during riots. Bills and partisans were long poles with various types of metal heads designed to cut, slash, and spear opponents, and could be used by the civilian watch as well as by trained infantry. The rapier was not the modern foil but a heavier, two-edged, pointed, and extremely lethal weapon favored by gentlemen and aristocrats. The Prince's train might be armed with partisans and know how to use them. In modern productions the actors may be armed with historically correct weapons, but they may also carry modern weapons which will determine how the fight proceeds.

77–99 'Your lives shall pay the forfeit of the peace' Just as it matters how old Capulet and Montague are, so the age of the Prince will also have an effect on how we understand the action. Is his failure to end the feud partly the result of the inexperience of a young ruler, the weakness of a middle-aged ruler, or the declining power of an aged ruler, whose waning authority, or even indifference, is known to the two houses? When his first attempt to subdue the riot fails, the Prince asks 'Will they not hear?' (l. 79), providing evidence not only of the ferocity of the fight but of the fighters' devotion to the feud – or perhaps that his forces cannot easily subdue the fighters. The riot has brought out people from most social levels, and it is possible to choreograph the action to make the hierarchy visible by using an inverted V moving from the servants downstage to the Prince upstage. Or the fighters can mingle without regard for rank, producing an image of chaos. The Prince's demands that they cease 'on pain of torture' (ll. 82–4), and his description of the bloodied combatants (l. 82) suggests there may be serious wounds. In noting that this is the fourth riot, he justifies his stringent decree (ll. 92–93). If the fighters leave their weapons behind when they exit these can provide a cue for Romeo's 'What fray was here?' (l. 169).

When the Prince speaks of the brawl as 'bred of an airy word' (l. 85), he prompts us to ask 'What started the feud?' but the play never answers this question. What does Shakespeare achieve by never explaining the feud's origin? First, the absence of any explanation of the feud's origin means we cannot take sides. Second, since Capulet soon admits the families should be able to keep the peace (1.2.1–3), he implies that there is no longer anything serious at stake. Third, and perhaps most important, he ensures that we experience the feud as the younger generation does – as something whose origin does not matter but whose imperatives are not to be questioned.

100–55 'Black and portentous must this humor prove'   Montague wants to learn what is driving his son to cut himself off from his family, his friends, and the rhythms of his being (ll. 130–6), and his words suggest Romeo has become melancholy – a condition which, in the medical theory of the time, might lead to suicide. Does he show sympathy for his son's suffering or is he baffled by his lack of 'manliness' (Loehlin, 2002, p. 95), as if wondering why his son cannot be more like Tybalt? Does Lady Montague seem to support or dissent from his attitude?

SD 'Enter Romeo'   All three texts have Romeo enter while his parents and Benvolio are discussing his plight, and the dialogue makes it clear that not only do Benvolio and the Montagues see Romeo (l. 152) but that Romeo sees his father (l. 158). Does the actor enter slowly, lost in thought? When does he see his parents and his cousin? Does he try to avoid them? As with the first entrance of other characters, we will immediately notice how old he seems to be. While Juliet, as the Nurse explains in 1.3, is 13 years, 11 months and two weeks old, Romeo's age is not specified, but the range of ages cannot be very wide since a 30-year old Romeo, for example, would hardly seem to be an impetuous youth, and in our own time his love for Juliet would be problematic. In the eighteenth, nineteenth, and even early twentieth centuries, Romeo and Juliet were played by actors in their 30s, 40s, or 50s, but since the 1960s, with the wide-spread formulation of adolescence as a separate life-phase, with the emergence of unique teen-age cultures, and with the success of Zeffirelli's film (1968), there is a premium placed on casting actors who, even if they are in their early 20s, can project the energy, the impetuousness, and the physical elasticity of adolescence, as well as the sense of wonder that seems so central to first love.

156–220 'Here's much to do with hate, but more with love'   Having introduced the feud as the source of hatred in Verona, and shown that hate embodied in Tybalt, the play introduces the

contrasting figure of Romeo. 'What fray was here?' (l. 169) is probably
provoked by some sign of the brawl, whether that sign is discarded
weapons, traces of blood, or a wound to Benvolio. Particularly crucial is his riddling assertion that the fray is not only a sign of hate but
of love (l. 171), which poses a question we will only be able to answer
after the play is over, namely 'What *is* the relation of hate and love in
Verona?'

Does Romeo seem to be a healthy young man who is adopting the
conventions of Petrarchan love as a form of role-playing? Or does
he seem to be undergoing the painful turbulence of first love? In
the 1590s, if an actor had wanted to create a Romeo who was 'going
through a phase', the question 'Where shall we dine?' (l. 169) would
have provided an opening: it would have suggested that, since loss
of appetite was a symptom of melancholy, Romeo's melancholy cannot be profound (Levenson, 2000, p. 156). On the other hand, Romeo
can be an introspective young man whose intense suffering justifies
his father's fears. A key speech in creating a truly melancholy Romeo
is his confession in lines 193–4: if Romeo does project a real sense
of having lost a previously stable identity, he may seem impelled by
the fantasy that to find a woman to love and be loved by is a way
to crystallize a new identity. Whatever version an actor creates, his
speeches reveal that in Romeo's mind he and the lady he professes
to adore are enacting an English version of Petrarchan love. Educated
members of the original audiences would have recognized Romeo's
rhetorical devices – especially the use of oxymora and other forms
of antithesis (ll. 172–7) – as those used in love-sonnets, and those who
were not literate would soon learn from Mercutio that they were hearing examples of 'the numbers that Petrarch flowed in' (2.3.37–8). Does
Romeo take these phrases seriously or is he playing a game? Does
Benvolio take his condition seriously or mock it? What is evident is
the shared commitment to and delight in language-games which parallels, in a different register, the word-play with which the servants
begin the action.

221–34 'Be ruled by me; forget to think of her'   Benvolio proposes the conventional cure for unrequited love (l. 224) and Romeo's
reply is equally conventional, but the actors determine the conviction
with which each man speaks. How do they exit? Romeo's 'Farewell'
(l. 233) suggests he tries to leave without Benvolio, so that the latter

must follow or catch up with him, but he can also physically link himself to Romeo to indicate his care and concern. How they exit may establish a pattern for male bonding in the rest of the production.

Act 1, scene 2: Day 1, Sunday early afternoon

1–37 'My will to her consent is but a part'   Shakespeare juxtaposes the exit of Romeo with the entry of Paris, inviting us to begin comparing the two men who will be rivals for Juliet. Romeo has invoked Petrarchan love, but, after Capulet's comment indicating that he and Montague should be able to end the feud (ll. 1–3), he and Paris resume negotiating an arranged marriage. In this practice, the match was usually negotiated by parents – so Paris is either old enough to woo for himself or his parents are dead – who took into account factors such as rank, inheritance, and economic condition, while also seeking the consent of the proposed couple. Capulet's speech (ll. 9–19) indicates that his concern for Juliet's welfare is such that he is in no rush to have her marry, so it will be surprising when he later short-circuits the process. For the actor playing Capulet, a key choice will be how to balance the peace-seeking patriarch of the first two acts with the enraged father who appears in the third act when Juliet refuses to marry Paris. The script provides an opportunity for him to preview that rage when he suppresses Tybalt's plan to attack Romeo at the feast (1.4.167–205). Is the actor playing Paris younger than Romeo, the same age, or older? Does he seem appealing enough to be a genuine rival to Romeo? Is he seeking the marriage purely as an economic transaction, or does he – although apparently he has not yet met Juliet – display some romantic ardor? As he turns from negotiating with Paris to inviting him to his feast, we can hear that Capulet shifts into couplets (ll. 16–37), perhaps becoming more lyrical to celebrate his daughter, and that he continues to speak in rhyme as he orders a servant to deliver the invitations.

38–84 'I pray, sir, can you read?'   In his prose solo, the servant can elicit sympathetic laughter as he confesses he is illiterate and must seek assistance (ll. 38–44). As Romeo reads the list, the servant may perform some business, such as trying to memorize the names while counting on his fingers, and the humor may be amplified by the pace at which Romeo reads. When he reaches 'My fair niece Rosaline'

(l. 71) – it is an intriguing point that Romeo is already in love with a Capulet – he can stress the name, stop dead, or exchange a look with Benvolio before the servant invites them to attend the party (ll. 81–4), and they can also share a meaningful look when he reads the name of Mercutio. These are the first two accidents which seem to confirm the Chorus's claim that the lovers are 'star-cross'd', and as other accidents follow they raise the questions about the relation of chance and agency.

82–101 'At this same ancient feast of Capulet's/Sups the fair Rosaline' Benvolio echoes Capulet when he urges that they accept the servant's invitation (l. 83) and the fact that both men speak in rhyme underlines the fact that they are now speaking a highly conventional language, and may prompt the actors to emphasize their use of, and delight in, such artifice. Their use of rhyme also means that for a moment the men from the two houses are formally united. Finally, the scene-ending couplet with which Romeo proclaims that no other woman can surpass the beauty of or shake his devotion to Rosaline (ll. 103–4) prepares for the irony that his devotion is obliterated by his first sight of Juliet.

Act 1, scene 3: Day 1, Sunday late afternoon

The third scene re-introduces Lady Capulet and introduces Juliet's Nurse and Juliet – although given how subordinate she remains here it is not until the next scene that Juliet reveals much about herself. In this scene, as she performs one of the most famous monologues in Shakespeare, it is the Nurse who is the theatrically dominant figure. How old is the Nurse? For much of the play's stage history she has been played as an older or even an 'ancient', woman. However, given that it is only 14 years since her daughter was born and 11 years since she was Juliet's wet nurse, she should not be much more than 50 years old, and can be younger. Her speeches in this scene make it easy for the performer to create an energetic, earthy, exuberant, irrepressible companion for Juliet, but she can also project less appealing traits, 'including stupidity, self-centeredness, and tediousness, features that performances rarely highlight' (Kliman and Magnus, 2008, p. 17).

1–9 'Nurse, where's my daughter? Call her forth to me' Lady Capulet's first words establish her attitude to the Nurse and Juliet, who are named by function or in relation to her, even as her speech also directs attention to the question of the relative intimacy of the three women. This point is emphasized by a subtle joke, for when the newly-entered Juliet asks 'How now, who calls' the Nurse replies 'Your mother' (ll. 5–6). What causes Lady Capulet to recall the Nurse? Is it because the Nurse sulks at being excluded? Because Juliet silently pleads to have her included? Or because Lady Capulet feels uncomfortable introducing the serious and intimate topic of marriage to a daughter she does not easily connect with?

11–64 'On Lammas-eve shall she be fourteen' As G.R. Hibbard points out, the Nurse's 'tricks of speech' represent one of Shakespeare's great innovations in his use of blank verse: the defining elements include 'her love of minute circumstantial detail, her readiness to digress on to any side issue that may arise, her addiction to inset parentheses, her repetitions in her efforts to get back on course, her insistent and irrepressible bawdry, [and] her utter inability to tell a plain tale plainly' (1981, p. 125) – and these elements contribute to making her speech a rich source for comic performance. Her first words (l. 2) introduce the focus on sexuality which will pervade her speech, and it is an indication of their ambiguity that Levenson claims this oath shows the Nurse remembering her hymen as intact (2000, pp. 170–1) while Kliman and Magnus hear her as having lost her virginity by that age (p. 17). The first phase of her speech (ll. 14–22), in which the Nurse establishes that Juliet is two weeks away from her fourteenth birthday, is rich in comic possibilities. For example, when she mentions Susan, the Nurse can make the sign of the cross, but how she does this will determine if she seems to be feeling genuine emotion or going through an empty ritual.

Do the responses of Lady Capulet and Juliet suggest this is a story the Nurse repeats habitually? If so, do they seem to relish the story, to be bored, or exasperated? Do mother and daughter have the same or different responses? Does the interaction of the Nurse and Juliet suggest that, for the Nurse, Juliet has become her surrogate daughter? As she gains momentum (ll. 22–36), the Nurse recalls the infant Juliet's life with the Nurse and her husband as she describes the earthquake striking at the moment when she began to wean Juliet (l. 33). This is

an intimate image and at least one Nurse has reinforced this sense
of intimacy by making Juliet put her hand on her breast (Loehlin,
2002, p. 108). The Nurse makes another associative shift (ll. 37–50,
52–9), juxtaposing this memory with her equally vivid account of
her husband's bawdy joke about Juliet falling backward when she
becomes sexually mature (ll. 44–5) – and for auditors 'Jule' is indis-
tinguishable from 'Jewel'. The anecdote indicates her husband shared
the Nurse's own delight in sexuality. The joke is one the Nurse thinks
good enough to repeat twice more, and given that Lady Capulet (l. 51)
and Juliet (l.60) command her to stop, the audience can laugh with
the Nurse or laugh at her if they find her exasperating. As Sasha
Roberts points out, the Nurse's bawdy focuses on the woman as agent
in the act of making love (p. 90), and we will be alert to see how
Lady Capulet and Juliet respond. Do all three women, for example,
delight in this acknowledgement of female desire, agency, and pleasure? Do Lady Capulet and Juliet laugh at the Nurse openly or in
spite of themselves? If all three women share this delight, then this
scene establishes a female solidarity that also helps explain Juliet's
frank avowal of and efforts to fulfill her desire. If the three women
are united here, the scene also prepares us to perceive a correspon-
dence and contrast with the trio of men who appear in the next scene,
as well as preparing for the moment when the Nurse and Mercutio
express their contrasting visions of desire in 2.3. If Lady Capulet dis-
approves of the Nurse's bawdy, the focus will shift to how Juliet
negotiates the different attitudes expressed by her mother and surrogate mother. Does she, for example, have to stifle her own laughter at
the Nurse's bawdy? Does Lady Capulet show her disapproval through
extra-textual efforts, whether physical or vocal, to silence the Nurse?
Does she use a look to silence Juliet? Does Juliet seem to share her
mother's attitude or to have her own attitude toward and relation with
the Nurse? Does Juliet feel free to display her affection for the Nurse
openly or does she indicate it with gestures unnoticed by her mother?

65–96 'How stands your dispositions to be married?'   Even if
she enjoys the Nurse's delight in female sexuality, when Lady Capulet
finally gains control of the conversation (ll. 65–101), she speaks in a
much more abstract and decorous language, developing a metaphor
of the wife as the 'cover' for the 'book' as a means to emphasize the
status and wealth such a marriage can provide (l. 96) – and thus

may suggest something about the nature of her own marriage. How fervently does Lady Capulet propose Paris as a future husband? When Juliet indicates that marriage is something she has not dreamed of (ll. 67–8), is she being honest or being demure to demonstrate subordination to her mother? Does her mother perceive her answer as a form of obedience or does Juliet's restraint strike her as a form of resistance? When Lady Capulet announces that she was a mother when she was Juliet's age, which would mean she is about 28 years old (see Hosley, 1967), is this factually correct, or is she visibly older, so that her speech displays some vanity? Do either the Nurse or Juliet or both make or share any response to that vanity?

97–107 'No less, nay bigger – women grow by men' The scene closes with a couplet from Juliet's two mothers (ll. 106–7), so it is up to the performer to hint at what Juliet makes of their contrasting emphases on the profits, pleasures, and perils of marriage. Sprague cites an 1884 performance where, as she exited, Mary Anderson's Juliet indicated her excitement by making small dance movements with her feet (1963, p. 299).

Act 1, scene 4: Day 1, Sunday evening

For the fourth scene in a row Shakespeare introduces a crucial member of the younger generation, and another character who, like the Nurse, tends to dominate the scenes in which he appears. Mercutio – whose name 'connects him with both the complex god and the volatile metal' (Levenson, 2000, p. 179) – is as irrepressible and bawdy as the Nurse, but he is a quicksilver creature, whose barely-contained energy erupts in displays of wit and flights of fantasy, prompts intense, sometimes physical encounters with Benvolio, Romeo, and the Nurse, explodes in the duel with Tybalt, and, finally, subsides in the cascade of puns and curses that precedes his death. Brooke introduces Mercutio during the Capulet feast, when Romeo meets Juliet, and all three are seated at a table, with each man holding one of Juliet's hands (see Brooke, ll. 251–90, in Sources); and this scene, as Joseph Porter notes, offers a glimpse of a potential love-triangle in which the two men would vie for Juliet. Shakespeare, however, creates a situation in which Mercutio and Juliet form a triangle centered on Romeo, and embodies the tension between male friendship and heterosexual love prominent in Renaissance literature, explored in *The Two Gentlemen of Verona* (1988, p. 9), and dramatized in this play throughout the scenes between the young men. Mercutio is usually played as being Romeo's age or slightly older, but he has also been cast as a man in his late twenties or early thirties who, for whatever reason, chooses to spend time with adolescents. Whatever his age, and although he is related to the Prince and is invited to Capulet's feast, he is a key figure in the Montague cohort. He also serves as a counterpart to the Nurse in creating the play's comic energies and, like her, articulates ideas about heterosexual love that contrast with the ideas articulated by and embodied in the action of Romeo and Juliet.

As with the Nurse, nineteenth and early twentieth-century critics often perceived Mercutio as a character whose histrionic potentials escaped the dramatist's control, and they suggested, for example, that the Queen Mab speech was 'an outburst of poetry from the author put arbitrarily in Mercutio's mouth' (Goddard, 1951, vol. 1, p. 122). The text seems to direct a comic realization of Mercutio insofar as Romeo explains to the Nurse that his friend is someone who 'loves to hear himself talk, and will speak more in a minute than he will stand to in a month' (2.3.137–9), and from Garrick's adaptation onward Mercutio was usually performed as a comic figure. In the first half of the twentieth century there was a consensus as to how Mercutio should be performed, epitomized by Rosemary Anne Sisson's description of Edward Woodward's Mercutio (*Stratford-upon-Avon Herald*, 11 April 1958) as 'a young man overflowing with high spirits, who has the cheerful, aristocratic insolence of the Prince's kinsman and whose bawdy jokes never nudging, but wittily gay, are funny without offence' (Jackson, 2002, p. 95). But since Zeffirelli's 1960 Old Vic production and his 1968 film, actors have created, and scholars have explored, a more disturbed and disturbing Mercutio, who speaks and acts in ways that range from mildly offensive to explicitly misogynistic, and who often is homosocially or homosexually attracted to Romeo.

1–47 **'And it pricks like thorn'** Mercutio tries to undercut Romeo's love for Rosaline by projecting an anti-Petrarchan view which reduces love to sexual desire and the effect of the exchange depends on the tone adopted by Mercutio and the response of Romeo. Are they good friends who are simply teasing each other or is there an edge to Mercutio's teasing? In their punning exchanges about pricking love (ll. 17–26), does Romeo seem truly melancholy, or is their word-play a sign that his melancholy is only skin deep? Does Mercutio implicitly express his desire for Romeo? How strong is Romeo's affection for Mercutio, and is his interest in women drawing him away from his friend?

48–103 'O, then I see Queen Mab hath been with you' When Romeo claims his reluctance to go to the party is prompted by a dream (l. 48), he provokes a speech from Mercutio that is comparable to the performance of the Nurse in 1.3 in its length, distinctive style, exuberance, and impact on both on- and off-stage audiences. In the first phase (ll. 51–67), the appeal comes from the way Mercutio's imagination enables him to develop his fantasy of a miniature world in remarkable detail and the performer has dozens of ways he can embellish his words with physical gestures. As he moves into lines 68–86, the actor may well change his tone (and mimic the figures he describes) as he presents Mab as causing dreams which project the dreamer's desires and fears; and he may well address these lines directly to Romeo since they imply that Romeo's dream has no validity. Finally, as part of his ongoing mockery of heterosexual love, Mercutio satirizes women (ll. 86–93) as creatures who become 'women of good carriage' because their upright bearing is transformed into the horizontal posture they assume to bear their lovers – and then must also carry the child conceived with that lover. The speech can operate in many ways depending on how the actor builds it, who he addresses, and how those addressed respond. Does Mercutio address the whole cohort of young men, prompting them to respond with delighted laughter as their champion fantasist engages in another light-hearted exercise of wit? Does he enlist the group to support him in persuading Romeo to snap out of his melancholy? Does he mock Romeo because he takes heterosexual love seriously? Is Mercutio in control of his speech from start to finish, and his rhetoric aimed at a specific objective, or is he carried away by his own fantasy, especially in lines 86–101, into an altered state? The group's response can also move through different phases so that, for example, they can initially be entertained, then puzzled, and then disturbed as Mercutio seems to shift from delightful inspiration to imaginative intoxication to an out-of-control, even hallucinatory state. Is it exasperation at his friend's irrelevant discourse, discomfort at its pointed attack, or concern for his welfare that causes Romeo to interrupt Mercutio? Is there physical contact between the two men and, if so, who initiates it and how does the other man respond?

104–12 'Some consequence yet hanging in the stars'   Although Mercutio persuades Romeo to go to the party, he does not dispel the latter's dark premonitions (ll. 107–9). Does Romeo seem haunted by death even before he falls in love with Juliet? Does he have to make a strong effort to overcome what he takes to be the serious warning offered by his dream? Or does he finally seem to trust in the higher power he invokes (ll. 104–11), and exit with the same exuberance displayed by his comrades?

113–38 'We cannot be here and there too'   How the movement from the street to the interior of the Capulet house is managed depends on the nature of the theatrical space. In modern productions, the transition is frequently simplified, so that the maskers exit, the servants may or may not appear to set the new scene, the Capulet party enters, and the maskers join them. '*Enter all the guests and gentlewomen*' does not precisely specify who enters, but given who speaks and is spoken to in the scene, this group must include Capulet, his cousin, Tybalt, Tybalt's boy, the Nurse, Juliet, and at least the servant who does not identify Juliet when asked by Romeo (ll. 154–5) – all of which suggests there are now at least 16 people on stage. In addition, there are figures who do not speak but who may be present. Does Lady Capulet enter with Capulet or separately? Furthermore, while it seems unlikely that Paris would neglect the invitation by the father of the woman he hopes to marry, it is up to the director if he appears in this scene. Does Rosaline appear, and if she does appear does she act in such a way as to motivate Romeo to turn his attention elsewhere? Finally, nothing specifies when the musicians enter, how many there are, what instruments they play, or where they place themselves. It seems likely that on Shakespeare's stage they played in the gallery, but these choices will depend on the resources of the company mounting a production.

139–53 '*Music plays and they dance*'   This scene provides a counterpoint to the opening brawl since feasting and dancing served to create images of communal harmony, and masks could dissolve constraints separating different groups within a larger community. In this case, the scene can create an image of harmony by showing Capulet women dancing with Montague men – but that image can also be taken as a way of conducting the feud by other means. Capulet declares he is past his masking days (ll. 134–7) but does he open the dancing with his wife? Does Lady Capulet dance with Tybalt? If she is younger than Capulet, does their dancing suggest that she and Tybalt are attracted to one another? Is she on- or offstage when Nurse summons Juliet to see her mother (l. 224)? Does Juliet or does the Nurse dance with Tybalt, which might establish a direct relation between one or both women and Tybalt, and motivate their grief at his death? Perhaps the most intriguing choice is whether Juliet dances with Paris. If she does, then she has an opportunity to indicate that, for whatever, reason, Paris does not appeal to her, which makes her response to Romeo a more deliberate act. Does Juliet dance with Romeo, which opens up the possibility that they discover their attraction to and harmony with each other either even before they speak? (This choice might mean cutting Juliet's description of Romeo in line 245.)

154–66 'O, she doth teach the torches to burn bright!'   Romeo's rapt speech (ll. 154–64) announces his conversion even as he previews the religious metaphor he will develop to woo Juliet. How does the actor physically convey his experience of love-at-first-sight?

167–205 'This, by his voice, should be a Montague'   The fact that Tybalt identifies Romeo by his voice indicates that Romeo is masked, but it is up to directors and actors to invent a reason he can do so. In sending his Page to fetch his sword, Tybalt reinforces the idea that his identity comes from killing Montagues. The conflict between Tybalt and Capulet provides an opportunity to characterize both men even as it also introduces a crucial element of the plot. Does Capulet's favorable response to 'young Romeo' (l. 177) suggest that, were he not a Montague, Romeo might be a match for Juliet? If he seems to suggest this possibility, does he thereby intensify Tybalt's rage? Their quarrel escalates as Tybalt begs Capulet to let him attack Romeo and Capulet first displays his harsher side – but that harsher side can range from the bluster of a man who basically hates confrontations and is flustered by rebellion in his family (exemplified by Michael Hordern in the BBC production) to the ferocity of a domestic tyrant who will exert whatever force is necessary to maintain control (Paul Sorvino in the Luhrmann film). Certainly he is verbally demeaning, addressing Tybalt as 'goodman boy' (l. 190), a 'double-edged insult' which treats Tybalt as if he were a yeoman, not a gentleman (Levenson, 2000, p. 195), and a boy, not a man. If the Page arrives with Tybalt's sword, Capulet may have to exert physical force, making it more likely that his guests will notice that something is amiss, and explaining why Capulet intersperses his discouraging comments to Tybalt with encouraging comments to the rest of the guests (ll. 195–201) – and his rapid shifts between rage and good cheer can add another comic touch to the scene. How Capulet controls Tybalt will establish a baseline for the level of violence he exerts when he confronts the Nurse, his wife, and his daughter in 3.5. It is a performance choice whether Tybalt pretends to submit or lets his uncle see his submission is pro forma (ll. 202–5). Since his ominous, suspense-creating threat is followed immediately by Romeo's first words to Juliet, the action here produces the sharpest juxtaposition so far of hate and love.

206–24 'If I profane with my unworthiest hand/This holy shrine' From its first appearance in English in poems by Wyatt and Surrey, in Sidney's *Astrophil and Stella* (1591 and 1598), and, as some of the original spectators might have known, in sonnets by Shakespeare circulating in manuscript, writers employed the sonnet to produce powerful, complex lyrics exploring love. In the play, however, Shakespeare makes the sonnet an event which does not simply register the experience of the male lover but rather enables both parties to initiate their relationship through a 'spontaneous collaboration over a complex poetic form' (Slater, 1982, p. 84). The sonnet creates a rhythm which starts cautiously as each speaker performs a quatrain, accelerates as they move into one- and two-line exchanges, and culminates in a shared line. As they speak, Romeo and Juliet will be doing all they can to gauge the other's response by attending to face, gesture, and body language – a harder task for Juliet if Romeo remains masked.

In the first quatrain (ll. 206–9), Romeo introduces the religious metaphor that will be the vehicle by which they begin to create their love. Petrarch often presented Laura as a saint and himself as a pilgrim seeking that saint's favor, and Romeo's language is still Petrarchan. But because both pilgrim and saint are incarnate here, the elements

are in play in a way they are not on the page. Based on a speech from
1 Henry VI (V.iii.46–9), in which the Duke of Suffolk kisses his fingers and touches the waist of the princess he is wooing for his king,
Anne Pasternak Slater suggests that in the original production Romeo
kissed the fingers of his hand and placed that hand on Juliet's waist,
but many Romeos begin by attempting to kiss or kissing Juliet's hand.
Romeo offers a clever apology in which he proposes that, if his first
gesture is a sin, he will do penance with a second, more intimate, gesture. In her quatrain, Juliet picks up the metaphor even as she picks
up one of his rhymes while initiating one of her own (ll. 210–13), and
makes her own elegant riposte by accepting his touch but suggesting that their hands should meet to create a 'palmers' kiss'. She thus
tests whether Romeo will modify his behavior to fulfill her request
(ll. 214–17), so that he must make a new request before learning if his
prayer will be granted. Again Romeo modulates, noting the parallel
between their hands joined in prayer and his lips joining together
in prayer (ll. 218–19). Their growing excitement is signaled by their
shorter, more rapid exchanges, and by the greater risks each one now
takes. Thus when he makes his request, she promises that, having
moved him to action, she will not move away when he moves to kiss
her. When she completes her line, it is also the third time she has
introduced a potential new rhyme, and since it is also the thirteenth
line of their emerging poem, the challenge for Romeo, presuming he
is conscious of and wanting to create a sonnet, is to pick up the pun,
find a rhyme to complete the couplet, and complete his pilgrimage
with a kiss on the lips. In this first (or second) kiss, the lovers experience the electrifying jolt of physical connection which arouses an
impulse to renew this pleasure, demonstrating how gratified desire
prompts them to feel a seemingly insatiable hunger for that pleasure (Slater, p. 85). So Romeo invites Juliet to begin a new sonnet,
and Juliet, as she introduces the next rhyme, prompts him to initiate a second kiss (ll. 220–3): 'they split a single line between them,
its caesura marked by their second kiss' (Slater, p. 85). The form and
content of the sonnet and quatrain direct a scene in which two people rapidly grow surer of their ability to respond to the cues offered
by the partner: what the actors will supply is the rising energy that
expresses the excitement of discovering a true partner in this verbal dance, the sense of opening oneself to the other person – and,
perhaps, the momentary impulse to pull back from such a rapidly

intensifying commitment. Part of the brilliance of this scene is the way the dramatist uses a closed form to create a sense of open-ended dialogue. As their verbal play produces a poem and their synchronized movement produces erotic intimacy, Romeo and Juliet initiate a relationship undreamed of in their world.

225–40 'Is she a Capulet?/O dear account! my life is my foe's debt'   How does the actor express the rapid-fire shift of emotions at the shock of learning Juliet's identity? If he has raised his mask, then when Benvolio urges him to leave (l. 232), he can snap it back in place to hide his identity from Capulet and his turmoil from his friends. Ironically, Benvolio cures Romeo's love for Rosaline, but his cure intensifies his friend's 'unrest' (l. 233) and it will be up to the actor whether the joy of this new love erases his earlier foreboding or is still mingled with that fear.

241–57 'My grave is like to be my wedding bed'   Juliet's ironically mistaken comment (ll. 246–7) reveals a desire to be married of which she has previously given no verbal hint, and she indicates the intensity of her desire by saying she will die if she cannot marry her wooer. Is this something she has known or does this discovery surprise her? When she learns her wooer's name, Juliet, like Romeo (ll. 230–1), feels she is hostage to hate (ll. 251–4). In their nearly identical one-and-a-half line speeches, Romeo and Juliet each connect their love with death, and the contemporary director can use lighting, blocking, or music to emphasize these parallel moments to underline the fact Romeo and Juliet are death-haunted from the moment they fall in love.

ACT 2

Sunday midnight to Monday afternoon

Act 2, Chorus 1–14 'Alike bewitched by the charm of looks'

The second Chorus would work better if the action was unfolding at the slower pace of Brooke's poem, but given that Shakespeare compressed nine months to just over four days, it makes sense that it is almost always omitted. This Chorus, too, is a sonnet and when it is performed the rhyme-scheme helps the audience follow the Chorus's explanation of how Romeo and Juliet will overcome obstacles that seem to insure they cannot meet again.

Act 2, scene 1: Day 1 – Day 2, Sunday midnight to Monday sunrise

1–7 'He ran this way and leapt this orchard wall'   When realistic settings were the unquestioned norm, Benvolio's words meant that there was likely to be a wall, and in nineteenth and early twentieth-century productions Romeo often did, and on film he usually still does, climb that wall. However, it is unlikely that such a property was originally brought on stage, especially since the mechanicals in *A Midsummer Night's Dream* are mocked precisely because they have an actor play the wall they do not trust their audience to imagine. Romeo probably withdrew behind one of the stage pillars, and if his friends stayed outside an imaginary rectangle formed by the pillars and tiring house façade, they would have reinforced a sense of two different spaces.

7–33 'I conjure thee by Rosaline's bright eyes'   As in his Queen Mab fantasy, Mercutio equates love with magic, announcing 'I must conjure him' (l. 17), playing with ideas of erection and resurrection – but the tone of the conjuration is open to a wide variety of performances from playful to harshly mocking. Roger Allam, based on his experience of playing Mercutio, suggests this speech 'is an attempt to call Romeo back both actually and metaphorically from danger' (p. 114). If Mercutio and Benvolio think that Romeo has entered the Capulet garden to meet with Rosaline, then Mercutio's speech may be an attempt to instruct Romeo what to do, but it may also be his attempt to humiliate Rosaline so as to prevent the sexual encounter Mercutio imagines taking place. In describing Rosaline, Mercutio produces a *blazon*, in which the speaker enumerates a lady's beauties – and a pattern Shakespeare satirized in sonnet 130 (see Sources). After citing Rosaline's forehead, eye, lip, leg, and foot, he celebrates the hidden parts of a woman's body (ll. 20–1), 'and he does so using a legal term that explicitly renders sexual possession as analogous to the ownership of property' (Callaghan, 2003, p. 18), extending his degrading depiction of women as objects. Mercutio, that is, presents male desire as nothing but sexual appetite and women as nothing but objects to satisfy that appetite.

34–43 'O that she were/An open-arse, or thou a popp'rin pear'   When Benvolio tries to get him to leave, Mercutio becomes more obscene, imagining Romeo wishing his mistress was 'an apple-like fruit' with the alternate name of 'open-arse', 'with allusion to female pudenda' (*Riverside*, p. 1113). Mercutio amplifies this image (ll. 38–9), invoking a pear that was thought of as phallic in appearance (Levenson, 2000, p. 206), and some scholars suggest the image here is one of anal sex, and may reveal Mercutio's desire for Romeo. It is striking that the elimination of these obscenities seems to have begun with the printing of the play: Q1 prints 'An open *Et cetera*', and Q2 and the Folio print 'An open, or'. Only in the 1890s did John S. Farmer and W.E. Henley, in *Slang and its Analogues*, propose that the phrase must have been 'open-arse'; only in his 1954 edition did Hosley make this emendation; and only after 1960 did actors playing Mercutio begin to speak this speech (G.W. Williams, 1964, p. 114). Here Mercutio, for example, can use his own and Benvolio's bodies as props, and if the two men are played as inebriated the scene can become adolescent jesting. But he can also be extremely brutal, as happened in the 1973 Royal Shakespeare Company production directed by Terry Hands, where 'Bernard Lloyd's misogynistic Mercutio . . . dismembered a life-size female doll with obscene violence as he enumerated Rosaline's body parts' (Loehlin, 2002, p. 130). From our point of view, his attack is misguided since Romeo's 'old desire' is dead, yet the fact that his love for Rosaline has been vaporized by his love for Juliet may also seem to validate this attack. Consequently, Mercutio's vision can also function to frame the next part of the scene as a moment in which Romeo will discover whether his new love will evaporate or flourish.

42–4 'He jests at scars that never felt a wound'   Although many editors follow Hanmer (1743–4) in imposing a scene break at the end of Benvolio's speech (ll.42–3), the fact that his last and Romeo's first line rhymed when the play was first performed has convinced most editors that originally there was no such break. Romeo is clearly responding to Mercutio's taunts and, whether he is bemused or offended, he makes a claim that this time the wound inflicted by love registers something very different from what he felt for Rosaline – a claim that is immediately tested.

45–75 'It is the east the Juliet is the sun' In the original production, Romeo would have turned from his departing friends and toward the tiring-house gallery to begin what has become known as 'the balcony scene', although none of the three texts ever uses this phrase and scholars have suggested that what the original audiences saw was Juliet at a window, lit by a candle. For much of the play's history, however, from the mid-eighteenth until well into the twentieth century, there has been a balcony for Juliet to stand on – and sometimes for Romeo to reach. The scene develops a strong rhythm, moving through five segments: the first two consist of Romeo's soliloquy and Juliet's overheard soliloquy; once Romeo announces himself to Juliet, they move through three segments created by Juliet's twice-performed exit-and-return, each segment ending with a short solo by Romeo.

Romeo's speech is a soliloquy insofar as he speaks with no one onstage who is aware of his presence or can hear him. Initially (ll. 45–52), he still speaks in Petrarchan hyperboles and paradoxes as he sees the light from what proves to be Juliet's bedroom as an emblem of Juliet herself. Which word or words does the actor stress? 'It *is* my lady' because he did not really expect to see her? 'It is *my* lady' because he is still stunned by the fact that, Juliet, unlike Rosaline, seems to reciprocate his love? 'It is *my lady*' because he is already utterly devoted to her? His rhapsodic outburst as he tries to learn more about her feelings for him prompts him to oscillate between the impulse to reveal himself and the fear that self-revelation will shatter the moment. When he wishes he was a glove on Juliet's hand (ll. 68–9), his conceit can gain force if Juliet's 'Ay me' makes it seem as if she were responding to his imagined touch.

76–92 'What's in a name?' Juliet's famous question raises profound issues about the relation of names and things, but for her the question expresses what she thinks is a simple desire not to be constrained by her family identity. Juliet believes, or wants to believe, that names are, to use a modern locution, arbitrary signifiers, attached to individuals merely by social and linguistic convention. Her question is ironic insofar as her speech resonates with the name 'Romeo' repeated six times at the beginning and toward the end, and thus echoes the 'Romeo' that resonates earlier in this scene (ll. 3, 8, 38, 40). These echoes highlight the fact that, whereas Mercutio's conjuring fails, Juliet, in a sense, *does* conjure Romeo, for what makes him announce himself is the sound of her voice invoking his name and promising that if he gives up his name he can 'Take all myself' (l. 92). Her unequivocal declaration puts Romeo in the intoxicating situation in which he can be sure of being loved before taking any risk himself. Her speech triggers a cascade of mutual responses which move at the breath-taking speed with which first-love often seems to sweep past obstacles, and much of the meaning of the scene will come from the pulsing energy of the actor's bodies and the tension between the desire to touch and the distance that prevents them from touching.

92–127 'Art thou not Romeo and a Montague?'   Romeo's ardent vow to be 'new baptized' (l. 93) not only accepts her unwitting offer but presents his fantasy of a phoenix-like death-and-rebirth in which his socially constructed identity can burn away. It is matched by Juliet's fantasy that she can marry him and follow him through the world (ll. 190–1). During much of this segment (ll. 92–184), the lovers create a new counterpoint as Romeo continues to speak in hyperbolic terms while Juliet reminds him that 'the place [is] death' (l. 107), so that her speech expresses as much anxiety for his safety as love for his presence. Just how anxious is Juliet? Are her warnings pro forma or does she genuinely fear for Romeo's safety and look around the garden? Are there any sounds that might signify a threat? How they speak and how their bodies move – the ardor with which they reach toward each other – will continue the process of developing a deeper harmony together even as they are, in most productions, prevented from completing that harmony in a physical connection.

128–84 'Thou knowest the mask of night is on my face'   Like Romeo earlier, Juliet now moves rapidly through a sequence of varying emotions, expressed in voice, gesture, and movement. She makes it clear that, although she has inadvertently violated decorum by declaring her love, she will only be won by an equal commitment (ll. 128–32), and is prepared to let their love be tested by time (ll. 164–5). Modern audiences tend to laugh when Romeo asks if she will 'leave me so unsatisfied' (l. 168) because they hear a sexual meaning, and this meaning will be especially prominent if Romeo has managed to climb up close to or onto the place where Juliet stands. In response to her question, Romeo's explanation (ll. 169–70) can be the clarification of an ambiguous question or an effort to offer an innocent sense for what was an implicit proposition. He elicits the intoxicating speech in which Juliet seems to sweep aside her own reservations, declaring that her love is 'infinite' (ll. 176–8) and thereby expressing, as Niamh Cusack, who played Juliet in the 1986 RSC production, has written, 'the joyous side of her personality' (1988, p. 123). Left alone, Romeo expresses both his delight in a dream come true and his fear that this dream will deliquesce. Much of the power of this scene comes from the exhilaration each lover experiences as he or she throws aside restraint in the whole-hearted expression of love, and from the oscillations they move through, as Romeo expresses his love but fears this moment may be a dream, while Juliet expresses her love but fears this moment may produce a nightmare of betrayal. While we can appreciate these oscillations, we can also recognize that their love seems as agonizing as it is wondrous precisely because they have no prior experience to help them find their bearings in the new world they seek to enter as they attempt to escape the world of the feud.

185–203 'Thy purpose marriage' When Juliet returns, the directness of her proposal can be as breath-taking to the audience as it is to Romeo – but the fact that she proposes so suddenly can make modern spectators wonder if something happens while she is offstage, just as it prompted Niamh Cusack to imagine 'that when she goes off to have that quick word with the Nurse, pressure must be put on her about the marriage to Paris; that would at least explain the complete change in tone, speed, and rhythm when she comes back and becomes so urgent in her talk of marriage to Romeo' (p. 127). But Ann Jennalie Cook points out that for the original audiences there would have been another explanation, based on the fact that an arranged marriage moved through a series of steps which required a contractual agreement as to the bride's dowry and the groom's jointure and at least the partial payment of both items; the reading of the banns three times in church; the performance of a church ceremony; a feast; and the consummation of the marriage. While the commitment became firmer with each step, it was not irrevocable until the final step was completed. Cook suggests that the crucial moment in this scene comes

onstage, not off, when Juliet says 'I have no joy in this *contract* tonight'
(l. 160, emphasis added). Here, she argues, Juliet 'assumes that with
their mutual declaration of love, Romeo has made a private promise
to marry her' (1991, p. 208) – so the proper question is not 'Why
does Juliet propose marriage?' but 'Why does she accelerate the process?' On Cook's reading, however, Juliet provides an answer for this
question also (ll. 193–5): she seeks to insure she will not fall victim
to the situation Ophelia sings of in 'Tomorrow is Saint Valentine's
day' (*Hamlet*, IV.v.48–66), where a young woman has sex with her
lover only to be told that, following the cruel (il)logic of the double
standard, he rejects her because she has been unchaste. Whatever off-
stage event we imagine might motivate Juliet to propose marriage,
one clear motive is to regain the control she inadvertently lost when
Romeo overheard her declaration of love.

204–31 'By the hour of nine'   After they complete the plan to
arrange their marriage (l. 214), Juliet's admission that she cannot
remember why she summoned Romeo (l. 216) is likely to prompt
sympathetic laughter. The image of Juliet as a spoiled child and
Romeo as a pet she might cherish to death (l. 229) can suggest how
close Juliet is to her pre-adolescent self, and Peggy Ashcroft, in John
Gielgud's 1935 production, was praised for her presentation of Juliet
as being both a child and a young woman. In their first scene, Romeo
and Juliet create a sense of insatiable desire by beginning a second
sonnet the instant they complete the first. Here, in Juliet's famous line
about the sweet sorrow of parting (l. 230), the lovers create that sense
by finding it nearly impossible to separate. If Romeo has ascended or
attempted to ascend to Juliet, he will need to return to earth even if he
is still walking on air.

232–35 'Hence will I to my ghostly Friar's cell'   As he announces
he will visit his 'ghostly father', not only does Shakespeare make it
clear that Romeo will be sleepless in Verona for a second night but he
illustrates the forces impelling adolescents to seek surrogate parents:
although Romeo could guess that his parents would love to hear good
news from their melancholy son, their joy might be short-lived if they
learned that the woman he plans to marry is the Capulet heir. So it
is logical that he decides to share his news with the Friar and his exit

offers another chance for the actor to express his joy in physical action that signals his sense of liberation.

Act 2 scene 2: Day 2, Monday dawn

1–30 'Two such opposed kings encamp them still . . . grace and rude will' Whereas the Nurse and Mercutio are introduced through vivid monologues, the Friar is introduced through a 30-line soliloquy as he gathers the plants from which he makes his remedies. There is, of course, no indication of setting beyond the plants and basket he carries, nor is it even necessary for him to collect any plants while onstage, although this is frequently done in modern productions and films. Simply through speech and action the Friar indicates that he is situated at a remove from the city, living closer to '[t]he earth' (l. 9), and perceiving the cycle of generation, death, and regeneration on a daily basis. In this soliloquy, he articulates a vision of human existence in natural and religious terms, and he is the only figure in the play who offers such a vision. As the play unfolds, he is seen in relative isolation for six of his eight appearances, four at his cell (2.5, 3.3, 4.1, and 5.2). Only in two late scenes (4.4 and 5.3) does he appear in a more social context, at the Capulet house and at the tomb. Given these parameters, the Friar can be played in a spectrum that ranges from presenting him as a figure whose detachment is a source of compassion and wisdom to one whose isolation makes him willing to take extreme risks with the lives of others. How old is the Friar? While he speaks of himself as old and nearing death in the last scene (5.3.267), he can be played as a middle-aged man or as one nearer in age to Romeo and Juliet than to Capulet and Montague. In recent productions there has been a tendency to cast him as a man in his forties or even his thirties and, therefore, someone who might be more in tune with the younger rather than the older generation.

When does Romeo enter? Q2 directs him to enter at line 22, so that he is present during and may overhear the end of the Friar's speech as he meditates on the fact that the same plant can have both medicinal and lethal properties (ll. 23–4) and works out an analogy to the individual human being, who has the capacity to choose between 'rude will' and 'grace'. But if the Friar has seen Romeo enter, it is also possible that he intends Romeo to overhear his discourse. Alan Dessen suggests that if Romeo enters here, the effect may not be so much that he overhears the Friar but rather that he becomes an illustration of the Friar's homily (1995, p. 66) – as he will vividly illustrate this struggle between grace and rude will when he confronts Tybalt's challenges in 3.1.

31–56 'I have forgot that name and that name's woe'   We will hear that the Friar speaks in couplets, that Romeo proceeds to speak in couplets as well, and that each man sometimes completes a couplet started by the other, suggesting that, just as he and Juliet were in harmony so he and the Friar are in harmony. Does the Friar take five couplets to work out the conclusion that Romeo has spent a sleepless night (ll. 33–42) because he is a laborious speaker? Or is this a moment in which they play a recurrent game, in which the Friar tries to guess 'What is Romeo up to *now*?' In some productions, the playful nature of their relation is indicated when Romeo completes some of the Friar's sayings. When the Friar's questions compel Romeo to realize that Juliet has obliterated all thought of Rosaline, he can register real shock, underlining the ironic reversal of his declaration that nothing could alter his love for Rosaline (1.2.103–4).

57–84 'Holy Saint Francis, what a change is here!'   This line usually elicits laughter because it highlights a truth Romeo has ignored, but it also marks the moment when the Friar begins to test the reality of this new love. In the couplets in which he works out a critique of male fickleness (ll. 66–80), does the Friar tease Romeo about his faithlessness for the sheer fun of teasing him? Or does he want to compel him to confront a serious point? When the Friar pretends to notice the 'stain' of an old tear on Romeo's face (ll. 75–6), do his words prompt him to touch Romeo's cheek, establishing a physical intimacy between them?

85–94 'To turn your households' rancour to pure love'   Does the Friar instantly conceive of the idea of using the marriage to end the feud or does he pause to think through his answer? In both Zeffirelli's and Luhrmann's films, the Friar resists the idea until he encounters what he takes to be a sign that the marriage might be sanctioned by God. To modern audiences seizing this opportunity may seem like a brilliant way to resolve the feud, especially since the idea that people should marry for love has become a premise that seems a natural, not a socially created, imperative. For some members of the original audience, however, the Friar's plan would have seemed a reprehensible subversion of the father's right to arrange a marriage. And while he sagely concludes by counseling caution (l. 94), the Friar undercuts his words by his decision to marry the lovers at once. Part of the complexity of Shakespeare's tragedies in general and of *Romeo and Juliet* in particular comes from the way that a maxim proposed by a character is tested by that character's actions and, in turn, that character is tested by his or her adherence to or deviation from the maxim.

Act 2, scene 3: Day 2, Monday midday

Like 1.1, this public scene moves through phases signaled by the entrances of the major characters, and accelerates the movement toward a comic resolution of the tensions prompted by the feud. What do the actors make of the fact that the scene is largely in prose, even though the young men and Nurse have previously spoken verse?

1–35 'More than Prince of Cats' As the scene progresses, the pattern of ironies initiated at the Capulet party intensifies since Romeo's friends still have no idea that he and Juliet have fallen in love and Romeo has no idea that Tybalt has sent a challenge. Mercutio insists that in pining for love rather than simply treating Rosaline as a sexual object Romeo has made himself unfit to meet Tybalt in a duel (ll. 12–16), and the actor can use these speeches to express Mercutio's resentment that love for Rosaline is emasculating Romeo. At the same time, in mocking (and, perhaps, imitating) Tybalt, he seems to satirize the opposite extreme of a man whose only interest is fighting. Mercutio's intense hostility can be played as hate at first sight, perhaps prompted by the fact that, however skillful he is, his punctilious style shows Tybalt to be a man who follows a rigid technique rather than being, like Mercutio, a brilliant improviser. Mercutio's description of Tybalt as 'Prince of Cats' – a play on Tybalt's name (Levenson, 2000, p. 228) – sets up his comment that he wants to take one of Tybalt's nine lives (3.1.76–7).

45–95 'Now art thou sociable, now art thou Romeo' For Shakespeare's first audiences, Mercutio's mocking enumeration of the heroines of famous love-tragedies (ll. 40–2), would have under-lined two ironies: first, that Mercutio is still ignorant that Romeo now loves and is engaged to Juliet; and second, that as the Chorus has announced, this pair will, like their renowned predecessors, die trag-ically. For modern audiences, however, for whom Juliet and Romeo have become *the* canonical example of doomed lovers, the speech functions as unwitting prophecy.

When we read the scene, we can use the notes to work out the details of the wit-combat (ll. 44–94) in which the two speakers make pun after pun after pun as each tries to top the other. But labori-ously working out the puns does not produce much laughter for readers and is not an option for spectators. Directors and actors have developed several tactics to deal with this problem. They can, like Garrick, cut almost the entire segment (ll. 52–94), leaving only the short exchange about straining courtesy before the Nurse enters, and this has been a frequent solution. Or they can focus less on com-municating the content of the exchanges and more on playing that combat with such high spirits that the audience shares their pleasure. Or they can physicalize the exchanges: '[i]n Peter Brook's production Romeo and Mercutio actually fenced with rapiers during the duel of wits; Romeo disarmed Mercutio at' line 65 (Loehlin, 2002, p. 151). In such performances audiences will recognize that Mercutio concedes Romeo's triumph (ll. 64–7) and they will grasp what Mercutio is cele-brating (ll. 84–5), namely that the love-sick Romeo has been replaced by the energetic, witty, 'sociable' (l. 84) Romeo whom Mercutio val-ues so highly – without any idea that it is being loved by Juliet that has produced this restoration. Finally, it is also the case that talented actors can convey the wit of this scene, enabling audiences to share the delight that is one of the highpoints in the comic first half of the play.

96–151 'A bawd, a bawd, a bawd!'   When the Nurse enters to arrange the details for the lovers' marriage, she underlines the fact that Mercutio has got it backwards when he asserts that Romeo seems to be his sociable self again because he has given up 'groaning for love' (ll. 83–4). At the same time, the meeting of Mercutio and the Nurse presents a clash of contrasting visions of love. In calling the Nurse '[a] bawd' (l. 122), Mercutio is unwittingly correct insofar as the Nurse is there to arrange a meeting between Juliet and Romeo, but he is wrong since that marriage will unite people who share an exalted vision of romantic love.

When Romeo signals the entrance of the Nurse by crying 'A sail! A sail!' (l. 96), he usually calls attention to some part of the Nurse's costume – for example, the huge veil warn by Pat Heywood in Zeffirelli's film – and Mercutio may not only mock the Nurse but seize or toy with some part of her clothing. Perhaps because she is appearing in public to speak to a gentleman, the Nurse tries to present herself as something more than a servant: she enters with her man; she shifts into prose; and, despite her own love of earthy language, she takes offense or pretends to take offense at Mercutio's ribald way of telling time (ll. 106–7). Mercutio intensifies his mockery in his snatch of song (ll. 126–9), using a harsh simile in which he depicts the Nurse as a prostitute who, like a pie made of stale ingredients, would be chosen only by a man who could afford nothing else. Is Mercutio's purpose here simply a comic deflation of pretentious behavior, or is there genuine animus in his words and actions? To what extent does the Nurse perceive or fail to perceive the details of his sexually mocking speech, and what stance does she adopt? The pair can be good-humored, relishing the bawdy exchanges, although the Nurse will feel she must express outrage after he leaves. Mercutio can be good humored but the Nurse truly outraged. Or, as has happened in some recent productions, Mercutio can commit an act that comes close to sexual assault – in which case the Nurse can be outraged but not frightened or outraged and frightened, and our laughter may die at the threat of violence. The text seems to set limits since Romeo reassures the Nurse that Mercutio is harmless (ll. 137–9) – if Mercutio hears this he may be offended – but if Mercutio, or Mercutio and other young Montagues seem to pose a genuine threat to the Nurse, then Romeo's speech will seem heartless or the words of a man trying to disassociate himself from the misogyny of his comrades. There is often comic business with Peter, and the humor will vary depending on whether Peter is played as wittingly or unwittingly bawdy in assertions about his 'weapon' that echo the servants in 1.1.

152–205 'And there she shall at Friar Laurence' cell/Be shrived and married' Here, perhaps because he is speaking of Juliet, Romeo shifts into verse (ll. 168–70 and 173–80) and thus may speak more lyrically as he gives instructions (ll. 162–80). There is often business when Romeo offers and the Nurse refuses but finally accepts payment (ll. 170–2). The odd exchange about the letter 'r' (ll. 195–9) is extremely hard to convey to modern audiences and is often cut. The scene can end with more business between the Nurse and Peter, which can restore a lighter comic tone if the Nurse has not been too severely attacked, or show the Nurse taking out on Peter any abuse she has suffered.

Act 2, scene 4: Day 2, Monday early afternoon

1–16 'The clock struck nine when I did send the Nurse'   Since Mercutio has just told the Nurse it is noon (2.3.106–7) and the Nurse has started her return journey, Juliet's words (ll. 10–11) reinforce the sense of action taking place in real time. As her impatience mounts and she complains about how slow 'old folks' are (ll. 4–15), even an initially still Juliet is likely to express her frustration in rapid and abrupt movement – the movement of a young woman whose active nature must depend upon the assistance of others. In this she differs from the heroines of the romantic comedies who, by disguising themselves as young men, gain scope for action. The comedy reaches a climax when Juliet utters her complaint about old folks (ll. 15–16) just as the Nurse enters. This reverses the pattern with Romeo and the Friar, and can prompt suspicion that the Nurse complains about her aching body as payback for Juliet's derogatory remarks.

17–77 'Then hie you hence to Friar Laurence' cell'   The Nurse usually uses her complaints to extract a massage from Juliet, which increases Juliet's impatience, but may also be a moment where the two women physically express their affection for one another. As with the first scene between Romeo and the Friar, it is a performance choice whether this teasing is one-sided or mutual (the Nurse may signal 'Gotcha!' before she becomes serious) and what balance of exasperation and affection is apparent in their interplay. As Romeo shifts from prose to verse when he gives the Nurse instructions for Juliet, so the Nurse moves into verse as she informs Juliet of the arrangements Romeo has made. When the Nurse notes that Juliet is blushing (l. 70), her words invite her to touch Juliet's cheek, and that touch may express the delight she has voiced from the very first mention of marriage for her charge – but it may also express a wistfulness that comes from knowing their relation will change when Juliet is married.

Act 2, scene 5: Day 2, Monday afternoon

1–15 'These violent delights have violent ends'   The Friar's concluding words (l. 35) indicate the scene was originally staged outside his cell, but modern productions sometimes situate it in that cell, introducing the setting for the scenes in which he counsels Romeo (3.3) and Juliet (4.1). This setting can be created with an altar and cross or in greater detail, in which case its properties may suggest aspects of the Friar's character. As they wait, the men echo the exchange with which they concluded their first meeting (2.2.93–4): the Friar offers a balance of hope and fear (ll. 1–2) while Romeo speaks of a joy that nothing can diminish (ll. 6–8). Romeo's extravagant rhetoric provokes a mini-sermon from the Friar, echoing his earlier admonition by counseling moderation in love (ll. 14–15). The more forceful his attempt to restrain Romeo, the more flamboyantly Romeo can express his desire in exuberant speech and motion.

16–37 'I cannot sum up sum of half my wealth'   The Friar announces Juliet's entry in words that indicate how the sight of her elevates his spirit (ll. 16–20) as well as Romeo's, and while the first sentence is likely to be addressed to Romeo, the rest of the speech may, as John Russell Brown has suggested (1981, p. 53), be spoken as an aside. When he describes Juliet as one who can 'bestride the gossamers' (l. 18), he echoes Romeo's image of her as an angel sailing through the sky (2.1.74–5), but when he concludes by saying 'so light is vanity' (l. 20) he introduces a sense of sin that does not seem caused by anything the lovers say or do. His words prompt Levenson to speak of his 'short, ominous wedding sermon' (2000, p. 247), and the actor may find a way to indicate what has prompted his shift in tone.

The entrance of Juliet originally may have functioned to illustrate 'Too swift arrives as tardy as too slow' (2.5.15), especially in light of the Q1 text which directs '*Enter Juliet, somewhat fast, and she embraces Romeo*'. That embrace can be acted in various ways. Romeo admits he cannot fully express his feelings (ll. 24–9), while Juliet echoes her earlier claim that her love is 'infinite' (2.1.178). The Friar's concluding speech (ll. 36–7) often serves as a cue for stage business in which he keeps or pries the young lovers apart, and the exit can prompt expressive staging: 'Zeffirelli [in his Old Vic production] had John Stride's Romeo walk backwards so that he continued to face Juliet, who was supported on the Friar's arm' (Loehlin, 2002, p. 164, citing *Shakespeare Survey* 15, 1962, p. 148). If the interval comes after this scene, it gives the audience time to savor the lovers' happiness and to experience the first two acts as a coherent event which fulfills the design of a romantic comedy – but even first-time spectators will know they need to brace themselves for tragic events to follow.

ACT 3

Monday afternoon to Tuesday sunrise

Act 3, scene 1: Day 2, Monday afternoon

For the third time, a scene opens by creating a sense that cohorts of young men are roaming the streets. The rhythm of the scene is created by the entrances of major characters, each entrance increasing the tension, which explodes into the lethal intimacy of the fights between Tybalt and Mercutio and Tybalt and Romeo, followed by the desperate appeals of the Capulets and the Montagues for the Prince to give judgment in their favor.

1–33 'For now, these hot days, is the mad blood stirring'   In the ominous heat of the day, Mercutio not only refuses to go indoors but, in another flight of fancy, mocks Benvolio as he had earlier mocked Romeo for *his* foreboding, outrageously describing him as if he were the Montague equivalent of Tybalt while denying his own quarrelsome nature. How anxious is Benvolio? How defiant is Mercutio? Does Mercutio resist simply because he refuses to be intimidated or because he is actively seeking an occasion to fight? Or because he is anxious to reassure himself that Romeo remains loyal to his male friends and has not been emasculated by love?

34–54 'Mercutio, thou consortest with Romeo'   As Mercutio baits him, Tybalt provides occasion for a quarrel in line 44. In the way he seizes on the ambiguity of 'consort' as 'associates with' and 'group of musicians' – as if Tybalt is designating both men as members of a class which includes vagabonds, minstrels, and, with meta-theatrical irony, actors – Mercutio can seem as eager as Tybalt to find occasion. As he says 'Here's my fiddlestick' (l. 47), does Mercutio point to, put his hand on, or start to draw his weapon?

55–71 'But love thee better than thou canst devise' Romeo does not know that Tybalt has sent a challenge to his home and Tybalt, like Mercutio and Benvolio, has no idea that Romeo has just married Juliet. When Tybalt calls him 'a villain' (l. 60), however, Romeo will instantly realize that Tybalt wants him to say 'Thou liest!' so he can respond with a formal challenge (Edelman, 1992, p. 178). Tybalt's words may well prompt a profound silence because 'The moment is, for Romeo, so packed with emotions that the actor may interpret it in half a dozen ways, each legitimate' (Granville-Barker, 1947, p. 309). At the same time, even the slightest pause will stun Benvolio, Mercutio, and Tybalt, since they will find it incomprehensible that Romeo does not produce the expected response. Instead, he makes a heroic effort to deny he is a villain without giving the lie so that he will not be forced to choose between fighting his wife's cousin and refusing to defend his honor. Does Romeo make his choice instantly or only after some inner struggle? When he calls Romeo 'Boy' (l. 65), mocking Romeo as Capulet mocked him in 1.4, Tybalt is posing a test like the one he posed when he called Benvolio 'coward' (1.1.68), and his demand to 'turn and draw' (l. 66) suggests that, as his 'farewell' (l. 64) indicates, Romeo has begun to walk away, as Benvolio may do in 1.1. Romeo's claim that he loves Tybalt (ll. 67–71) will further shock the other young men because in refusing to fight Romeo invites further humiliation. His situation embodies the truth acknowledged by Sir William Segar in *The Book of Honor and Arms* (1590), namely that every gentleman who adhered to the honor code while professing himself a Christian was caught in a dilemma (see Sources). Segar defined the issue facing Romeo when he explained that '*Cicero* saith, that he who repulseth not an injury, being able, offendeth no less, than if he had abandoned his friends, parents and countrie' (A2ᵛ). Mercutio may well take up the challenge because he sees Romeo as abandoning friends and parents when he refuses to repulse the injury.

72–108 'O calm, dishonourable, vile submission!'   While there
is no doubt about the indignation of Mercutio's first response (l. 72),
who he addresses and for what purpose is open. Does he address
this as a reproach to Romeo, perhaps to goad him to accept the
challenge? Or does he address Benvolio to express their shared bewil-
derment? Or is it addressed to Tybalt as he prepares to take up the
challenge? Edelman notes that the text offers implicit directions for
the Mercutio–Tybalt fight. First, when Mercutio says he will 'dry-beat'
Tybalt (ll. 76–8), he can be heard as challenging Tybalt to a non-lethal
encounter in which he plans to humiliate him by beating him without drawing any blood (p. 178). Second, given that Benvolio's later
report describes how Mercutio fought using both hands (ll.161–3),
the men must have fought with rapier and dagger. Third, our famil-
iarity with the play obscures the fact that members of the original
audience who knew Brooke's poem, 'while knowing that Romeo was
eventually to kill Tybalt, would have no reason to connect Mercutio
with that event, as Brooke does not place him at the scene' (p. 177),
and would have been stunned by Mercutio's death. Historically, this
fight has often been staged as a rapier-only combat, and with the
fighters out for blood from the start. The modern tendency is for
this to be the most extensive of the fights, with the men displaying
their prowess in high-risk moves and reversals. Frequently, Tybalt
performs as Mercutio suggests, fighting by the book, while Mercutio
displays the flair shown in his verbal duels: the fight director Malcolm
Ransom, for example, staged the scene with a 'punctilious Tybalt' and
a 'streetwise Mercutio', so that Mercutio took 'his wit into his fighting'
(Allam, 1988, p. 118). There are often reversals in which one man gets
the upper hand, lets his opponent escape, finds himself in jeopardy,
and recovers.

Q2 implies the fight begins after Mercutio delivers line 83, but
Edelman points out that a good deal of fighting may occur before
Romeo calls on Benvolio to intervene and attempts to stop the fight
(ll. 84–8), producing the moment when '*Tibalt vnder Romeos arme thrusts
Mercutio, in and flyes*' (Q1, Fᵛ). Key choices include how Romeo intervenes and whether Tybalt's thrust is accidental or deliberate. If it is
deliberate, especially if Mercutio has been holding his own or gaining
the upper hand, it will undercut Tybalt's honor and make Romeo's
revenge seem more justified. If it is accidental, it may seem another
instance of the lovers' star-crossed fate. Does Mercutio call for a

surgeon because he thinks his wound is not lethal or because he already knows it is serious? Does the fact that he calls for a surgeon but not a priest indicate that he hopes to survive or that he is indifferent to religion? If Mercutio knows his wound is fatal, does he hide this fact from his friends as part of his devotion to playacting and desire to maintain their admiration? Certainly if the actor pretends his wound is 'a scratch' his behavior helps explain the apparent levity of his friends' responses, mitigating what can otherwise seem callousness on their part (ll. 90–103). How enraged is he at Romeo, and how seriously does he utter his thrice-repeated curse? Does the fact that he asks Benvolio to help him off signal a repudiation of Romeo? Does he make some gesture before he exits to indicate that he forgives Romeo? Or does he come back on to make such a gesture? For the original audiences, 'A plague o' both your houses' would have recalled the horror of the pestilence that had decimated London in 1593–94 and closed the theaters for 18 months – and would foreshadow the decimation of the younger generation in this play.

109–36 'O sweet Juliet,/Thy beauty hath made me effeminate'
While Romeo is willing to endure the disgrace entailed in refusing to accept Tybalt's challenge, his agitation here comes from the fact that he now confronts a double dishonor, for not only has Mercutio died seeking to maintain Romeo's honor but Romeo has inadvertently contributed to his death. 'The news that Mercutio is dead completes Romeo's total absorption into the avenger-role prescribed for him in the code of honor, the role from which he had earlier distanced himself so carefully' (Snyder, 1996, p. 94). In many productions this is a shorter, more violent fight, in which Romeo may find himself about to be killed and succeed either by accident or because he becomes possessed by such fury that he overwhelms Tybalt. In despairingly crying out that he is 'fortune's fool' (l. 136), he suggests he is fortune's plaything because in trying to avoid a tragic dilemma he impales himself on both horns, one after the other.

137–97 'And for that offense/Immediately we do exile him hence' Again the Citizens enter, again they may appear as officers of the watch, and again it is a performance choice as to how many there are, how organized they seem to be, and how quickly they gain control. The speed with which they arrive is indicated by the fact that they have heard of the killing of Mercutio, but not of Tybalt. Do two citizens speak, each asking a question, perhaps supporting each other, perhaps at cross purposes? Does one citizen speak and does he command the others? Certainly one citizen exercises authority when he commands Benvolio to follow him (l.140). How and in what order do the Capulets, Montagues, and the Prince arrive? Does the blocking echo the opening scene? In a production that wants to stress the intractable nature of the feud, the Capulets and Montagues could enter before the Prince and resume full-scale combat, which would indicate that they are *not* intimidated by the Prince's decree. Again, the size of the Prince's train is important for establishing his control. How enraged is the Prince? How vehement is he in silencing Lady Capulet and Montague? Does he have to silence other would-be speakers? Given how the fights have been staged, does Benvolio's account (ll. 152–75) seem impartial? Or is he downplaying how much Mercutio provoked Tybalt? One choice that will indicate Benvolio's honesty will come at the end of his speech to the Prince (l. 174): does he point in the direction of Romeo's flight or does he point in another direction? Does he show any signs of uneasiness that he did not intervene, or is his final offer to be executed if he is distorting what happened (l. 175) convincing? Why is it Lady Capulet, not Capulet, who twice speaks for her family? Is this because Lady Capulet is the dominant partner? Because Capulet has reservations about Tybalt due to his propensity for violence? The five 'O's in her first speech (ll. 146–50) suggests she is extremely vehement, and her vehemence may prompt her to kneel by or even hold the corpse of Tybalt, in which case she may rise with blood on her clothing, on her hands, or on her face. Her second speech, without any 'O's, may be calmer, but she remains firm in demanding Romeo's execution (ll. 176–81). In productions from Garrick onwards (1748) these speeches were usually spoken by Capulet, but in recent productions, especially those which show Lady Capulet to be attracted to or even having an affair with Tybalt, having her deliver these lines enables her to express the depth of her attachment. In such stagings, the reaction of Capulet can be revealing. His silence, for example, can indicate ambivalence about this death, either because Tybalt's propensity for fighting made him difficult to control or because he has been cuckolding Capulet himself. In Bogdanov's 1986 production, Capulet slapped Lady Capulet across the face as she made her plea (Jackson, p. 56; see Key Productions). Having listened to Benvolio (ll. 152–75), Lady Capulet (ll. 146–50, 176–81), and Montague (ll. 184–6), the Prince knows he must enforce his ultimatum to insure the families take his decree seriously. He lets Romeo live but exiles him, adding he will be executed if found in Verona (ll. 194–5) – and when he pronounces this sentence Lady Montague frequently becomes grief-stricken, which may prefigure her offstage death. Opposed in life, in death Tybalt and Mercutio together have begun to transform a romantic comedy into a romantic tragedy. Finally, unless there is a curtain, the scene must conclude with the removal of Tybalt. If Mercutio has died onstage, or if his body has been brought out to lie with Tybalt's, then it makes sense for some of the Prince's men to remove the body of his kinsman. If Lord and Lady Capulet have been accompanied by the young men who entered with Tybalt earlier in the scene, they can be the ones to remove his corpse. A highly ceremonious exit will prepare for how the director stages the final scene.

Act 3, scene 2: Day 2, Monday afternoon

Just as Shakespeare transforms the sonnet from a lyric to a dramatic event so here he transforms the epithalamium, or nuptial song:

> [p]rothalamium and epithalamium were part of the ritual celebration of a marriage, offered to the bridal pair by a poet, an allegorical figure, a chorus, but not spoken by the bride herself. But for Juliet there can be no public celebration (5–7). That she must speak her own epithalamium emphasizes her aloneness, the need for secrecy to which both she and Romeo must submit.
>
> (Clemen, 1987, p. 97)

A modern audience may miss key features of Juliet's epithalamium. First, a man – whether the poet or the husband – should address the bride. Second, the bride 'is supposed to weep profusely to demonstrate her modesty' (McCown, 1976, p. 165). Third, this wedding song is another step in the lovers' effort to perform as many of the marriage rites as possible within the limits imposed by a clandestine ceremony. Juliet composes her own poem, serves as speaker and addressee, and expresses a whole-hearted desire to lose her maidenhead in order to achieve erotic pleasure and complete their marriage. She thus continues to violate the decorum supposed to govern her actions, but the speech is designed so that the actor can express herself in a manner that will make her seem innocent but not ignorant, chaste but not coy, frank but not bawdy. 'Surprisingly, given the histrionic opportunities it provides Juliet, this scene was cut entirely in some Victorian productions', and even when not omitted it 'was regularly edited for content until the twentieth century; lines 8–16, with their sexual explicitness, were almost always cut' (Loehlin, 2002, p. 176). Victorian-era critics such as Halprin, Massey, and Lamartine confronted a dilemma: they either had to condemn Juliet or, as Lamartine did, defend her from the charge that 'the most scandalous obscenity usurps the place of . . . virgin purity' (Furness, 1961, p. 440). Modern Juliets, by contrast, often perform the whole speech and may perform overtly erotic gestures or movements as they speak.

1–31 'Come night, come Romeo, come thou day in night'   In her previous soliloquy Juliet was awaiting news, but this time she is waiting to make love with Romeo, and her desire will be registered in the way imperatives saturate and animate her delivery: '[w]ithin thirty lines Juliet employs no fewer than eleven imperatives: "Gallop . . . Spread . . . come . . . learne . . . Hood . . . Come . . . come . . . Come . . . Give . . . Take . . . cut" ' (McCown, p. 153). The momentum of her aria prompts her to leap from sexual 'death' (orgasm) to literal death, summoning night to immortalize Romeo, and the hyperbolic image suggests the actor's delivery may be quite extravagant as she indulges her fantasy (ll. 17–25) – and this intensifying energy will feed her impatience with the Nurse.

31–69 'Is Romeo slaughtered, and is Tybalt dead?'   While we may share Juliet's exasperation at the Nurse's speeches, because we know the facts we can focus on the impact of her words on Juliet. At first, the mistaken belief that both Romeo and Tybalt have died produces insistent punning on 'I', 'aye', and 'eye', until the Nurse finally clarifies the situation (l. 69). Juliet's use of puns in such a tragic situation has prompted directors from Garrick onwards to cut these lines, and many literary critics have agreed these puns and conceits seem highly inappropriate for a person in such distress, but some Juliets have made them work in expressing the way the tragic dilemma drives her to distraction. The actress will decide how extreme Juliet's loss of control is here, and that loss of control will set a threshold for the rising emotion when she drinks the potion and when she wakes to discover Romeo's corpse.

69–89 'Shame come to Romeo!' Levenson argues that Juliet's word-play is the means by which Shakespeare dramatizes the shock of someone for whom 'grief has arrested her imagination', and before she musters the resources to craft a coherent response (2000, pp. 58–9). As Snyder notes, 'Her shock at suddenly having to superimpose Romeo the murderer on Romeo the lover is certainly real, but its articulation through neat oxymora . . . makes clear that she is speaking as a generic Capulet' (1996, p. 95). The Nurse's attack on Romeo may seem shocking to us, but it foreshadows her later counsel that Juliet marry Paris.

89–107 'Blistered be thy tongue/For such a wish!' As will happen in 3.5, a short speech by the Nurse operates as a catalyst, provoking Juliet's fierce response (ll. 90–1); and the fact that she completes the Nurse's line suggests she should respond instantly. It will be up to the performer to find a way to indicate when and how Juliet discovers the consequences of her commitment to her husband: 'Lucy Whybrow [in Noble's 1995 RSC production], shrieking and hysterical before, stopped cold with this line, her sudden realisation giving her a new maturity' (Loehlin, 2002, p. 180).

108–26 'Tybalt is dead and Romeo banished' The fact that Romeo is banished (l. 112) hurls Juliet into despair, with the word *banished* tolling five times in 13 lines (ll. 112–24) and providing the performer with a cue for how to build this speech (ll. 125–6). If earlier the lovers seem to express insatiable passion, Juliet now expresses a sense of infinite loss, and her desolation will be in stark contrast to her elation moments earlier – the emotional extremes being another way the actor can register her adolescent nature.

127–43 'I'll to my wedding-bed,/And death, not Romeo, take my maidenhead' Juliet again equates sex and death as she composes a revised ending for her epithalamium, in which death replaces Romeo as her lover (ll. 136–7) – an echo of her words when she feared that the man courting her at the dance might be married. The Nurse's promise (l. 140) revives Juliet's spirits, and when she exchanges the ring for Romeo for the cords she takes another step in her effort to complete their marriage. Holding the cords may induce a lightening of her spirit expressed in an energetic exit.

Act 3, scene 3: Day 2, Monday afternoon

Much of the power of a Shakespeare play is generated by the sequence of scenes even as their meanings are created by juxtaposition, which Granville-Barker calls the playwright's 'chief technical resource' (p. 308). In case spectators miss the connection between 3.2 and 3.3, when the Nurse enters she remarks that Romeo 'is even in my mistress' case' (l. 84). Their parallel responses emphasize their similarity as well as how separation increases their suffering.

In this scene the age of the actor playing Romeo comes to the fore since one question raised by this scene is 'How much can a Romeo cry without forfeiting his manliness?' (Jackson, p. 131). In the nineteenth and much of the twentieth century, Romeo's grief has seemed *un*manly, creating a dilemma for actors who seek to fulfill the text's mandate. Romeo's collapse needs to be severe in order to create a contrast with his response when he hears of Juliet's death, yet the sight of a 30 or 40-year old man collapsing is likely to seem ludicrous. However, if Romeo is played by an actor who is or seems to be in his teens, his reaction can seem acceptable as the regression of someone who is still an adolescent. The nature of his collapse here will also influence our sense of whether Romeo seems to have matured by the end of the play.

1–70 'Not body's death, but body's banishment'   How does Romeo react to what the Friar thinks is the relatively good news of banishment? Does his response indicate surprise because he was expecting a sentence of death? Or does he instantly feel that being banished is worse than death? His words (ll. 12–13) catch the Friar off-guard, and after he makes one forceful speech (ll. 24–8), Romeo's passion leaves room only for short interruptions. Juliet spoke of banishment five times in 14 lines. Romeo repeats some form of 'banished' 14 times in 56 lines, and the actor can use the word to shatter each consolation the Friar offers until Romeo collapses (ll. 69–70).

71–107 'In what vile part of this anatomy/Doth my name lodge?'
Having symbolically tried to bury himself, Romeo refuses to hide
when they hear knocking at the door. The seven dashes inserted in the
Friar's speeches by modern editors such as Levenson and Evans suggests a performance in which the he oscillates with near-comic desperation between the door and Romeo. Having admitted the Nurse,
he seems to turn this problem adolescent over to her (l. 83), and while
she may be more sympathetic she, too, seeks to make Romeo rise
to his responsibilities as a man (ll. 88–90). Inadvertently, however,
she provides the cue for his suicide attempt when she describes how
hearing of Tybalt's death and Romeo's banishment prompted Juliet's
collapse (ll. 101–2). Earlier, Romeo offered to be 'new baptized' (2.1.93),
and said of his name 'Had I it written, I would tear the word' (2.1.100).
Since that ecstatic moment, however, Romeo has undergone a painful
education in how names inscribe definitions, and in his question to
the Friar (3.3.104–6) he suggests only radical surgery can excise the
identity which seems to insure the end of his marriage just hours after
it was solemnized.

Most Romeos do not succeed in wounding themselves but recently
some have (see Paparelli's staging in Key Productions). Q2 directs that
the Friar stop Romeo, but Q1 directs that *'He offers to stab himself, and
Nurse snatches the dagger away'* (G1ᵛ), and Dessen suggests that 'The playgoer who sees Romeo's self-destructive violence interrupted … by
the Nurse and then hears the Friar's terms (e.g., "Art thou a man?";
"Thy tears are womanish"; "Unseemly woman in a seeming man") is
therefore encouraged to consider: what kind of "man" *is* Romeo at this
point in the play?' (1995, pp. 92–3).

107–57 'Take heed, take heed, for such die miserable' At 51
lines, Laurence's speech is longer than any soliloquy by Juliet or
Romeo, but is often substantially cut. Uncut, however, it enables a
talented actor to develop a carefully orchestrated plea which also
provides time for Romeo to regain his composure. Robert O. Evans
notes that this speech is the Friar's supreme effort, and that while in
previous scenes he has relied on the persuasive force of aphorisms
delivered in sententious couplets, here he is compelled to muster
all his resources to create a detailed argument that can persuade
Romeo to abandon suicidal despair (1966, p. 54). The actor builds an
impressive argument which moves through a series of four steps.

'Art thou a man?' is a question which can emerge as early as 1.1 if Montague is worried about his son's manliness. It becomes explicit when Tybalt calls Romeo 'Boy', and when Mercutio's death makes him proclaim that loving Juliet has made him 'effeminate'. Now his suicide attempt prompts the Friar to make the same indictment, but what will be crucial is the attitude the actor projects: does he mainly express his own shock or is he trying to shock Rome? Is he simply outraged or is there compassion as well as outrage? How much physical contact does the Friar use not only to keep Romeo's attention but indicate his love for his 'son'?

As he develops his three-point rebuttal (l. 121), the Friar revives an analogy he employed earlier when he reminded Romeo that 'These violent delights have violent ends,/And in the triumph die like fire and powder,/Which as they kiss consume' (2.5.9–11). Now he presents the image of an unskillful soldier trying to charge a matchlock but injuring himself by igniting the powder prematurely (Gibbons, 1980, p. 181), suggesting that Romeo is misusing his gifts to ignite a self-destructive emotional fire. As the Friar argues that the things Romeo sees as a cause for despair are better seen as blessings, he makes his argument easy to follow because as he enumerates each item he concludes 'There art thou happy' (ll. 136, 137, 139) – and this explicit, climactic sequence can make it easier for Romeo to regain his self-control. The repetition in line 144 invites the Friar to speak with particular force as he foresees that a tragic ending has become more probable. Hoping he has restored Romeo's manhood, the Friar urges him to take positive action, even though this action will cause further pain since the pleasure of making love to Juliet will be followed by separation. As is always true of such long speeches, it is in part the evolving responses of the addressee, as well as of any onstage witness, which determines how we understand what the speaker is doing, and the success of the Friar's performance will be established by the nature of Romeo's recovery.

158–64 'How well my comfort is revived by this'   The Friar's speech enchants the Nurse, whose praise of learning (l. 159) can prompt our laughter, either expressing delight at her sincerity or a rueful sense that learning has its limits. Changes in Romeo's posture, expression, and tone will signal how the gift of the ring coupled with the prospect of making love with Juliet completes his recovery, and leads directly to his reconnection with the Friar.

165–74 'It were a grief so brief to part with thee'   If the Friar has been the one to disarm Romeo it may be here that he returns the dagger, perhaps with some byplay in which Romeo assures him he will not try to kill himself again. How do they perform their farewell? Is Romeo so focused on Juliet that he starts to rush off and the Friar must call him back (l. 171)? Or does Romeo want reassurance, which the Friar initiates by a handshake? Does that handshake turn into an embrace? Or is it the Friar who needs reassurance that his harsh rebuke has not alienated Romeo? While Romeo exits re-energized, hopeful, and eager to make love with his wife, the Friar, although he too may be hopeful, may also express how much this encounter has cost him by some non-verbal action that releases the tension he has experienced.

Act 3, scene 4: Day 2 – Day 3, Monday evening to Tuesday before dawn

1–11 'That we have had no time to move our daughter'   Hardly has Romeo left to climb to Juliet's bedroom than Capulet, Lady Capulet, and Paris enter, forming an ominous constellation. But the first part of the scene seems reassuring as Capulet explains why Juliet will not come down (ll. 1–5), and as Paris starts to leave we will start to breathe a sigh of relief.

12–35 'Sir Paris, I will make a desperate tender/Of my child's love'   In Q1 there follows '*Paris offers to go in, and Capulet calles him againe*' (G2ᵛ), and this direction highlights the fact that the director can increase the suspense by letting Paris reach a door, perhaps even open it, and by having Capulet and Lady Capulet also come near to completing an exit before Capulet recalls him, underlining the way he makes another impulsive decision which contributes to the destruction of those he seeks to marry (ll. 12–14). When Capulet instructs his wife to prepare Juliet for the wedding to his 'son' (l. 16), his word reveals that in his mind Paris is already his son-in-law, and the actor playing Paris may indicate his excitement at his new status – although sometimes Paris initially seems nonplussed by the haste before expressing his delight (ll. 20–9). Original audiences would have known that Capulet was ignoring essential steps in arranging a marriage, and would have recognized that betrothing Paris and Juliet would create enormous pressure in any case, but that setting the wedding for Thursday increases it exponentially. Because Capulet does not consult his wife, the open silence makes it possible that she non-verbally dissents from his decision. Finally, Capulet's plan creates a looming tragic dilemma for Juliet even as his order for his wife to visit their daughter creates suspense as to whether she will find the lovers together. Michael Boyd (RSC 2000) directed a striking ending to this scene: 'Capulet and Lady Capulet kissed tenderly at the end of the scene, while Romeo and Juliet appeared and kissed on the balcony above them; a poignant juxtaposition' (Loehlin, 2002, p. 192). Such a juxtaposition highlights the irony that Capulet is promising Juliet to Paris at the moment when she is completing her marriage to Romeo, and thus also highlights the way Shakespeare anticipates the split–screen effect in film.

Act 3, scene 5: Day 3, Tuesday dawn

This scene initiates a sequence of events extending to the end of Act 4, during which Juliet goes from lying in bed with her husband to lying dead in the Capulet tomb. In this scene alone, Juliet says farewell to Romeo, enrages her father by refusing to marry Paris, and resolves to commit suicide if the Friar cannot prevent this marriage.

As discussed in the first chapter, this scene probably worked by having Romeo and Juliet enter above, with Romeo descending by the rope ladder down the tiring house façade and Juliet descending inside the tiring house, to reappear on the platform, bringing her bedroom with her. The image of the lovers aloft will provide a powerful contrast to the first balcony scene: there, they are unable to reach each other, while here, having achieved union, they must separate. (In productions where Romeo does climb the balcony in 2.1, the scenes become more nearly parallel.) Modern productions often place Juliet's bedroom on the main stage and have Romeo disappear from the back of the stage. In terms of indicating what the lovers have been doing, while Zeffirelli's film (1968) caused a sensation with glimpses of each lover naked, by the time Adrian Noble directed his

RSC production in 1995 the lovers could appear naked in bed (Loehlin, 2002, p. 193).

1–63 'O, think'st thou we shall ever meet again?'   In this scene, Shakespeare continues to experiment with lyric forms used for dramatic purposes. He transforms the *aubade*, a poem spoken by lovers lamenting how dawn cuts short their joyous time together (see 'Break of Day' in Sources). Once again he energizes a form by having both lovers speak, by having them speak while threatened with exposure and, for Romeo, execution, and by having them argue whether it is dawn. This is another scene in which the actors will express the volatile shifts of emotion in the lovers, who often move in opposite directions, registering the ongoing tension between delight and agony that is central to their experience. So, as Katherine Dalsimer notes 'Juliet is always at odds with time, imploring it to go faster or slower' (p. 80): whereas in two of her earlier soliloquies she implores time to go faster now she wants to slow it down. Indeed so powerful is her desire to stop time that at first she seems ready to sacrifice future for present happiness as she insists that Romeo stay (l. 16) – and Romeo seems to accede to her request (l. 19). On the one hand, Romeo reaffirms a claim he made in the orchard (2.1.118–21), namely that life without Juliet is not worth living. On the other hand, since he admits he will be lying when he agrees with her, Romeo prompts us to ask if this speech is a genuine affirmation of his willingness to die or a way to make Juliet realize he must depart without appearing to be ungallant. His words and the use of her name – one of the few times he addresses her by name – jolt Juliet out of her wishful thinking, so that she reverses the imperatives of her epithalamium as she commands 'Hie hence, be gone, away' (l. 26). After completing their marriage, the liminal state of the lovers is registered in the change from night to day, in Romeo's descent from high to low, and in his flight from Verona to Mantua.

64–125 'The County Paris . . . / Shall happily make thee there a joyful bride'   In this segment of the scene, our response is shaped in part by the fact that daughter and mother are each one-up and one-down: Lady Capulet knows of Juliet's betrothal to Paris and Juliet knows of her marriage to Romeo. Lady Capulet first tries to comfort Juliet in an unexpected manner, assuring her that she will send someone to Mantua to poison Romeo (ll. 78–92) – a plan which may register the vehement devotion to revenge she displayed in pleading with the Prince to execute Romeo. Her threat prompts Juliet to utter equivocal statements which Lady Capulet hears as supporting the murder of Romeo but which we know are Juliet's covert affirmation of her love for him (ll. 81–3, 85–6, 93–102). Directors frequently cut these speeches, eliminating what used to be thought of as an unlady-like vengefulness on the part of Lady Capulet and an unlady-like equivocation on the part of Juliet. If these speeches are spoken, however, they are another moment where the characters reveal the deforming pressure of the feud. Only after elaborating her revenge plot does Lady Capulet inform Juliet that she is to marry Paris on Thursday (ll. 112–15). Like the Friar sharing what he believes is good news, Lady Capulet, who may reach out physically to share the joy, is stunned when Juliet vehemently rejects the marriage. Juliet's use of stichomythia (ll. 114–17) – in which her rejection parallels yet reverses Lady Capulet's phrasing – emphasizes that she has never responded to her mother in such a defiant manner.

126–95 'An you be mine, I'll give you to my friend'   When he enters, Capulet still sounds like the caring parent of earlier scenes, but once he realizes Juliet will not consent his rage becomes so intense that Lady Capulet (ll. 156, 174) and the Nurse (ll. 167–8, 171, 172) protest, and are silenced by his counter-attack. A blustering Capulet will intimidate them simply by his patriarchal authority, but a truly violent Capulet – one who assaults one, two, or all three of the women – can create such visceral fear that whole scene can seem balanced on the edge of a knife. Even a blustering Capulet is shockingly harsh as he warns Juliet that if she does not comply he will treat her as if she were a criminal being taken to execution (ll. 147–56); that if she does not marry she should never see him again (ll. 159–67); and that if she does not consent he will turn her out to 'die in the streets' (ll. 175–95). His harshness is emphasized by the fact that even when Juliet kneels (ll. 156–7) she cannot move him – or may move him to strike her. Capulet, then, seems to lose control of his temper as he realizes he is losing control of his hitherto obedient daughter, and it is possible that the blocking here may recall how he disciplined Tybalt in 1.4 – not knowing that Tybalt was already planning to disobey his command by challenging Romeo, as Juliet is planning to disobey him by preserving her marriage to Romeo.

196–203 'Do as thou wilt, for I have done with thee'   Lady Capulet apparently hears Juliet's threat that she will die (ll. 200–1) as hyperbolic and like her husband cuts off further appeals (ll. 202–3). Does she coldly dismiss Juliet? Or does her husband's attack leave her so shaken that she does not really hear Juliet's threat? Is it the case that, however much she cares for her daughter, there is no way to support her against the authority of her husband? When her mother rejects her appeal, does Juliet collapse, as she did when she learned of Tybalt's death and Romeo's exile? Many Juliets weep, but the performer may also display a new resolve as she moves toward a resolution to die if she cannot prevent the marriage.

204–34 'Amen'   Juliet turns to her most trusted ally but the text indicates the Nurse is slow to respond. A pause after line 209 is optional, but it seems that Juliet must pause after line 211 before asking again for 'comfort' (l. 212). The Nurse's silence may suggest her distress in being forced to choose between her surrogate daughter and her employer. Her speech advising Juliet to marry Paris comes as a shock to Juliet and may well shock first-time spectators (ll. 212–25). As Anthony Dawson notes, we will be compelled to ask

> where does her betrayal of Juliet, her total failure to understand this girl she has nursed since infancy, come from? Somewhere in the earthy garrulousness so comically endearing throughout the first half of the play, there has to be a hint of the insensitivity, the hard practicality, that emerges [here] hardly an hour after Romeo has left, when the Nurse advises Juliet to forget him, and commit bigamy by marrying Paris.   (1988, p. 132)

For much of the play's history, the Nurse's advice has been the counsel of a survivor adjusting to her own and Juliet's dependant states, but if, as has become more common, the Nurse is conflicted, the actor will need to find a way to convey her struggle, and decide whether it is visible only to the audience or to Juliet as well. One quiet but wrenching moment comes when Juliet says 'Amen' to the Nurse's vow that her advice comes from both her heart and her soul (ll. 226–9). The Nurse's 'What?' can be a request for clarification by someone who does not hear anything untoward in Juliet's pious word or the distressed reaction of someone who understands that Juliet is cursing her. Juliet, however, retains or regains enough self-control to offer a misleadingly reassuring explanation and to announce she will go see the Friar (ll. 232–3). If the Nurse recognizes that a gap has opened between them, that recognition can induce great distress, which she may display as she exits from the scene. But her final speech (l. 234) can indicate that the Nurse decides not to disrupt their apparent harmony.

234–42 'If all else fail, myself have power to die' As in 3.2, the Nurse prompts a tectonic shift, registered by Juliet's startling 'Ancient damnation' (l. 235), as she discovers that her loyalty to Romeo demands that she reject the Nurse. This is often seen as another moment in Juliet's maturation but it is also the case that she is doing exactly what her parents just have done, namely make an all-or-nothing choice. In this soliloquy, the change in Juliet will be expressed by the fact that in this suddenly somber situation she does not speak in her earlier rhapsodic manner but uses plain language to express certainty about her potentially lethal course of action. Desperate as she may be, Juliet's speech and movement can convey that, while she is trapped by her father, abandoned by her mother, and betrayed by the Nurse, she is also liberated, free to act for herself and in defense of her marriage. Her energy is likely to rise as she plans to visit the Friar, hoping he can find a remedy but prepared to kill herself if he cannot (l. 242). Her words echo Romeo's suicide attempt, yet the plainness of her speech contrasts with the extravagance of his. If Romeo's isolation from his family is signaled by the fact that he never sees them after the first scene, Juliet's alienation from her family is highlighted by the fact that she must fight to preserve her integrity while in their midst. At the end of Act 3, then, the lovers embody the gender-inflected external and internal forms of exile children can undergo during adolescence.

ACT 4

Tuesday midday to Wednesday sunrise

Act 4, scene 1: Day 3, Tuesday midday

1–17 'her father counts it dangerous/That she do give her sorrow so much sway' Friar Laurence's opening dialogue with Paris establishes the location of the scene and the fact that it is now Tuesday. The explanation Paris offers for Capulet's haste (ll. 6–10) shows Shakespeare transforming his source, for in Brooke Juliet's incessant weeping prompts her mother to infer that Juliet is jealous that other young women are already married. In the source, therefore, her father seems to be making a match as much for his daughter's benefit as to fulfill his own agenda. Paris can deliver line 15 with anything from respectful humility to offended superiority, insulted that the Friar should ask any questions at all, and the performance choice will help shape our attitude toward Paris.

18–43 'Till then, adieu, and keep this holy kiss' When Juliet enters, Paris expresses delighted surprise but Juliet must try to conceal the fact that at this moment he is the last person she wants to meet. How successful is Juliet in hiding her dismay? Is Paris's insistence on eliciting a confession of love and securing a kiss the result of his love coupled with an assumption that Juliet is reticent from modesty? Or does it come from a need to claim possession of his prize? Or is he so insistent precisely because he senses her resistance? His persistence compels Juliet to engage in the sort of equivocation she employs when responding to her mother's idea of poisoning Romeo (3.5.78–103), and here again directors often shorten or omit this word-combat. Juliet's maneuvers seem like the parrying of someone who wants to end a duel without wounding and without being hit, and her question (ll. 37–8) provides an adroit end to their fencing. Nonetheless, Paris insists on kissing her (l. 43), using words that ironically echo the 'holy palmers' kiss' Romeo won from Juliet.

44–126 'Be not so long to speak; I long to die' The Friar's admission that he has no solution for Juliet's dilemma (4.1.47) provokes a response he clearly is not expecting as she pulls out a dagger and threatens to commit suicide (ll. 50–67). His expression is likely to convey 'Not Juliet too!' and, depending on how she handles the weapon, she may or may not convince him that she is ready to kill herself now. It is also possible that when she reminds him that he married her to Romeo (l. 56) she may stress 'by thee' to threaten him with exposure. In the Luhrmann film, Claire Danes pulls out a gun and not only points it at herself but at the Friar, threatening him not merely with exposure but death. Whatever the specific threat she makes, her action registers how the feud keeps securing new recruits and new victims.

Does the Friar have the mixture prepared, and if it is prepared does he have it on his person? Or must he invent the idea and prepare the potion on the spot? If he does have the potion ready and on his person, he can trade the vial for Juliet's weapon. If he must make the potion from scratch, then the tension can be prolonged through the preparation. The Friar explains his plan in two phases. During the first phase (ll. 68–76) he offers the gist but not the details, and his speech seems to function as a dare – a dare Juliet rises to in lines 77–85. As with Romeo in 3.3, it is a choice whether her response seems to be the over-the-top reaction of someone maddened by the trap she is in or the factual claim of someone who believes she can endure anything to maintain her integrity. In the second phase (ll. 89–120), as he explains the details of his plan, the Friar seems to be both calming down an overwrought girl and offering instructions to a maturing young woman, and Juliet may oscillate between these two states. If the Friar has managed to get her weapon from Juliet, he probably returns it here – and again, as may happen after Romeo's departure from his cell, the Friar may show how the steadily worsening situation is taking a toll on him even as he continues to believe they can solve the challenges they face.

Act 4, scene 2: Day 3, Tuesday afternoon

1–14 'So many guests invite as here are writ'   Once again Capulet cheerfully invites guests to a party whose arrangements he is supervising, and his banter with the servant echoes his banter at the earlier feast. Although he speaks critically of Juliet (l. 13), his tone may indicate that his rage has dissipated.

15–47 'I'll have this knot knit up tomorrow morning'   For Capulet, Juliet's submission (ll. 16–21) is a wonderful reversal, and he probably makes a gesture to indicate he pardons her, most likely during line 27, at which point Juliet can rise from her knees, and he may embrace her. When he praises Friar Laurence (ll. 30–1), Capulet's words will have an ironic ring to Juliet, perhaps to the Nurse, and certainly to us. Exhilarated by Juliet's submission, for the third time Capulet makes an impulsive decision that contributes to the tragedy, for in advancing the wedding to Wednesday he creates a situation in which the Friar has almost no time to inform Romeo of the new plan. This time, Lady Capulet does protest, although not about the marriage but rather the preparations (ll. 37–8). Capulet sends Juliet and the Nurse off, sends his wife to help them prepare, and bustles off, promising to stay up all night (l. 41) in a mood probably as exuberant here as he was enraged in 3.5. His final words (ll. 45–6) are not only ironic but will resonate when Romeo begins his scene in Mantua by making an announcement about his 'cheerful thoughts' (5.1.3–5). Both men will be elated shortly before learning of Juliet's death, and in both cases the news which shatters their elation will be false.

Act 4, scene 3: Day 3 to Day 4, Tuesday night to Wednesday dawn

1–5 'But, gentle Nurse,/I pray thee leave me to myself tonight'
Does Juliet speak as if their intimacy has been fully restored? Is the Nurse deceived by Juliet's apparent reversal or is she surprised and puzzled? If the Nurse seems convinced that all is well, her cheerful preparations for the wedding may elicit some pity for the shock she is about to endure. If she indicates that she is puzzled by this change, she will show that she can still read Juliet. When Juliet commands the Nurse to leave her alone (l. 2) does the Nurse's register any sense that this is their last moment together before Juliet moves to her new husband's home?

6–19 'Get thee to bed and rest, for thou hast need'   When Lady Capulet wishes her daughter 'Good night' she may speak to her with more tenderness than she has ever shown before (ll. 12–13). For both Juliet and us, 'Farewell' may have a poignant quality since Lady Capulet has no inkling that her daughter is planning a future in which she may not be able to see her family for a long time. How badly does Juliet lose her nerve here? Her desire to have the Nurse comfort her (ll. 14–17) may recall earlier moments when the Nurse has comforted her with a touch or an embrace. But line 18 also can be spoken with a harsh emphasis on '*she*' to acknowledge that the Nurse cannot be part of Juliet's plans since she cannot be trusted.

20–57 'My dismal scene I needs must act alone'   Loehlin notes that the 'potion scene' was for a long time one of the great set pieces in the standard repertory of an English actress, adding '[w]hile in the nineteenth century it was considered the supreme test of an actress's Juliet, its importance diminished in the twentieth' (2002, p. 214). The speech projects the oscillations Juliet goes through as she reaches the point of no return in carrying out the Friar's plan. The basic movement of this speech is created by the questions Juliet asks as she imagines the possible outcomes of the plan, but the tone, volume, and tempo of each phase depends on the performer, who must project the interaction of desperate hope, extreme terror, and logical argument that finally enables her to drink the potion.

As she examines the vial (ll. 20–2), the initial doubts she articulates are expressions of the same doubt: can she trust the Friar? More specifically, she asks 'What if the potion is a placebo? What if the potion is a poison?' For the first problem her remedy is the dagger, which she draws and places on the bed. She thus has within reach the means to rehearse death and, if that fails, to perform death. Juliet turns to the possibility that the Friar has given her poison to prevent exposure of his part in her marriage to Romeo (ll. 23–8). This is a logical fear since, if the plot is exposed, he will be revealed to have violated the rights of Capulet and Montague to control the marriages of their heirs; and indirectly to have contributed to the deaths of Mercutio and Tybalt and the exile of Romeo. This is a more threatening possibility, but Juliet reassures herself that his past actions have shown him to be trustworthy – although she tacitly admits this is only a probability (l. 28). Thus Juliet dismisses her first two doubts with relative ease, and may create suspense by starting to raise the potion to her lips before further doubts assail her.

The next two uncertainties, which emerge from realizing that even if the potion works there are other ways the plan could backfire, arouse true horror (29–35), and it is possible that each doubt from here to the end of the speech erupts as she starts to but cannot yet bring herself to drink the liquid. When she imagines the drug working, her words recall that, when the Friar first came up with the plan, she emphasized that she could 'without fear or doubt' (4.1.87) endure being shut in a charnel house with corpses and skeletons (ll. 81–7). But now she imagines the plan only partially succeeding, so that she wakes before Romeo can rescue her and that in the airless vault she will die an agonizing death from asphyxiation. Here, then, she acknowledges that the risks have been multiplied by the fact that she must take the potion 24 hours earlier than originally planned and the sense of these greater risks is likely to prompt a much more intense delivery.

Envisioning herself as asphyxiated seems to be a tipping point: Juliet becomes so agitated that her imagination shifts into reverse, and it can seem that terror may be about to overwhelm her capacity to reason, impelling her to move not toward but away from drinking the potion (ll. 36–53). The dashes inserted by modern editors suggest how she struggles to articulate yet defend herself against being overwhelmed by images of gothic horror, and they may also mark moments when she moves as a means either to express her terror or to try to escape it. Even without the dashes, however, the intensity of her resistance is registered by the fact that it takes her three tries before she can fully formulate the question (ll. 35, 44, 48), with each try again likely to be marked by an increasing desperation in speech and action. At this point, Juliet can seem so precariously balanced that neither the character nor a first-time audience may be able to discern if this internal debate will impel her to drink the potion or to abandon the plan. In a torrent of fantasy – which parallels Mercutio's Queen Mab fantasy but in a very different key – the balance tips again when Juliet hallucinates a scene in which Tybalt's ghost attempts to kill Romeo and she cries out 'Romeo, Romeo, Romeo! Here's drink – I drink to thee!' (ll. 55–8). Conjuring her husband apparently is the only way to overcome the ever-increasing horror which would otherwise paralyze her will to drink the potion, and his name seems as if it were a talisman to ward off destruction. Through its twisting syntax, start-and-stop rhythm, and clotted imagery, Juliet's speech invites each performer to create her own unique realization of this harrowing odyssey.

Q1 'She falls upon her bed, within the curtains'   As noted in Chapter 1, theater historians have proposed three options for the original staging, including a curtained bed thrust onto the stage, a bed located in the discovery space, or a curtained bed resting against the wall of the tiring house (Levenson, 2000, pp. 315–6). In contemporary productions how this scene is staged will depend in part on the nature of the stage itself. What does Juliet do with the dagger and the vial?

Act 4, scene 4: Day 4, Wednesday before dawn

'For fifty years, from the end of the nineteenth century some performances omitted the scene entirely' (Levenson, 2000, p. 316), and in
such productions the use of elaborate sets meant that it made sense
to eliminate a set-change that might have taken longer than the scene
to perform. On Shakespeare's stage the bed could have remained in
full view, and the Nurse would simply have moved toward it to wake
Juliet.

1–12 'The curfew-bell hath rung; 'tis three a' clock'   Capulet's
words (ll. 1–12) situate the scene in a night of hectic preparation which
ends with the arrival of Paris and the musicians, and it is noticeable
that time-markers appear with increasing frequency from now on,
emphasizing the quickening pace of action. Capulet's boast of being
able to stay up all night prompts a reply (l. 11) in which Lady Capulet
can assert that Capulet has been a 'pursuer of women' (Levenson,
2000, p. 317) – provoking an exchange which can be the teasing of
a loyal couple, the bitter accusation of a wronged wife, or a remark
whose sting is lessened because he did so before they married.

13–26 'The County will be here with music straight'   The sound
of off-stage music marks the arrival of the groom to serenade the
bride, and its harmonies will create dissonance for us since we know
that the family will soon find Juliet apparently dead. It is a choice
how long the music continues to play, hence how painful the effect of
'mirth in funeral' (*Hamlet*, I.ii.12) becomes for the Capulets and Paris;
and the moment when the music ceases will also have an impact.

26–42 'Alas, alas! Help, help! my lady's dead!'   As the Nurse performs her 16-line monologue – Hibbard wryly notes that 'No one
but the Nurse would take this long to find out what happened' (1981,
p. 128) – we anticipate the moment when she will discover that Juliet
is dead. Believing that, after consulting with Friar Laurence, Juliet has
decided to wed Paris despite the illegal and sinful nature of the act,
she speaks with the focus on sexual delight which has characterized
her from her first words about her maidenhead. Indeed this whole
speech complements her first summoning of her 'lamb' insofar as it
is saturated with her endearing names for Juliet. If the Nurse's first

monologue shows us two pivotal days in Juliet's life as a three-year old, this speech offers an image of how Juliet's days may have begun for the next ten years. When she warns Juliet she will have little sleep on her wedding night and then rebukes herself (l. 33), we cannot tell if she thinks she needs forgiveness for her bawdiness or because helping Juliet prepare for her first night with Paris reminds her of having helped her prepare for her first night with Romeo. Certainly as she fusses about the room her eager anticipation of the couple's lovemaking heightens the shock when she finally realizes that Juliet is dead. She must open the bed curtains by the time she speaks line 38, but may do so sooner, in which case the poignant effect of her direct address to Juliet becomes more intense – or her obliviousness more pronounced, or both.

17–42 'Death is my son-in-law, death is my heir'   The festive clothing worn by Paris will reinforce the dissonance created by the music. As the family and Paris learn of Juliet's death, they initiate the formal patterns of speech that dominate much of the scene. But before this happens, Capulet's speech to Paris (ll. 61–6) gains its impact by gathering up the series of moments when other characters, especially Juliet and Romeo, have made the connection between love and death. Capulet takes this conceit a step further when he announces 'Death is my son-in-law, death is my heir' (l. 64). Although he thinks death has pre-empted Paris, for us his words make Death the rival of Romeo. Capulet goes further (ll. 65–6) for he imagines the extinction of himself, his family and his house – which seems, in fact, to be their fate at the end of the play.

43–90 'Accurs'd, unhappy, wretched, hateful day!'   Summarizing a great deal of theatrical experience, Russell Jackson remarks that 'The stylized grieving of the Capulet family ... is one of the most intractable of the play's impassioned passages for the modern actor and director' (p. 172), so it makes sense that directors often cut some or all of this segment, as well as Peter's dialogue with the musicians. Garrick, in his 1750 revival, cut almost the entire scene and replaced it with a 'funeral procession of Juliet, in which the following dirge is sung' (5.1) to music composed by William Boyce. His version used the musical procession to create a solemn effect which simultaneously expressed yet contained grief. Intractable as it may seem, this does not mean this segment must be dismissed as unplayable. A pattern can be seen in the first line spoken by each of the four mourners:

Lady Capulet. Accursed, unhappy, wretched, hateful day! (l. 69)

Nurse. O woe! O woeful, woeful, woeful day! (l. 75)

Paris. Beguiled, divorced, wronged, spited, slain! (l. 81)

Capulet. Despised, distressed, hated, martyred, killed! (l. 85)

This seems to be a speech written for an operatic quartet in which the voices state, echo, and vary a theme. As Charles Lower has pointed out, Q1 offers a stage direction that 'All at once cry out and wring their hands', followed by 'All cry: And all our joy, and all our hope is dead,/Dead, lost, vndone, absented, wholly fled' (I2 ʳ), followed by speeches that differ from those in Q2. Lower suggests a performance in which Capulet speaks, then Lady Capulet, Nurse, Paris, and Capulet speak simultaneously. Whether or not they have been influenced by Q1, some directors have created analogous effects:

Terry Hands, in 1973, overlapped the several mourning speeches, treating them 'as a sort of fugue, the first speaker accompanying the second with repeated fragments of his theme as a counter-subject' (David, *Shakespeare in the Theater*, p. 113). He used the same business in 1989, setting up a definite rhythm in all the mourner's lines which the Friar then picked up for his speech as well, giving the scene surprising energy and pace. Adrian Noble also overlapped the mourning, making it a sort of round, whereby each speaker said the first line loud and at a normal speed, then continued in a slower, quiet voice as the others followed (RSC 1995). Michael Boyd rearranged the text to have Paris and Capulet alternate their words in their formal lament, suggesting a kind of competition in their mourning (RSC 2000). In the 1978 BBC-TV version, the mourning speeches are played naturalistically, with the close-up camera focusing on the different reactions of each speaker (Paris is cut). (Loehlin, 2002, pp. 224–5)

91–121 'The heavens do lour upon you for some ill' The Friar's seemingly conventional speeches (ll. 91–109, 117–21) produce disturbing ironies. On the surface, he offers standard forms of comfort for the family's loss (ll. 96–104). But even if this speech is delivered with utter conviction and succeeds in moving the mourners, the audience, like the Friar, knows that Juliet is alive and that his real purpose is to insure that Juliet and Romeo live 'married long'. The most disturbing moment may come when the Friar warns the family that Juliet's death is heaven's punishment for some unrecognized misdeed (ll. 120–1). Does this speech elicit some non-verbal reaction from the Capulets, the Nurse, or Paris? Does the Friar show any indication that he may well be wondering if the heavens are frowning on *him* for his rash attempt to end the feud? Does the Friar's attempt to make them believe that some sinful act of theirs has contributed to Juliet's death verge on cruelty? We will watch the Friar closely to see if he betrays any uneasiness here, even if we cannot be sure as to the specific cause of that uneasiness.

SD Exeunt all but the Nurse/124 'this is a pitiful case'   Levenson's direction here amplifies and clarifies Q2's '*Exeunt manent*' (K3^r) even as it shortens Q1's '*They all but the Nurse goe foorth, casting Rosemary on her and shutting the Curtens*' (I2^v) – a direction that corresponds with the Friar's direction to the mourners (ll. 105–6). The Q1 direction offers three interesting elements. It directs the mourners to cast rosemary on Juliet's corpse for remembrance; affords the Nurse a moment to mourn her beloved surrogate daughter; and, having opened the curtains, it provides her with the opportunity to close them. The Nurse's moment with Juliet's corpse may recall the fact that she has already lost both her daughter and her husband. It also provides a second moment when the Nurse can find the vial and/or the dagger and try to grasp their significance. It certainly is the moment for the Nurse to express her grief: 'Peggy Ashcroft recalled in the Oxford University Dramatic Society production in 1932, while playing the unconscious Juliet, she needed great concentration not to burst into tears when Edith Evans said, "this is a pitiful case" ' (quoted by Loehlin, 2002, p. 227).

96–146 'O, play me some merry dump to comfort me'   How was this concluding segment of the scene originally played? What function(s) did it perform? A clue to answering the first question comes from Q2, which prints '*Enter Will Kemp*' when Peter enters at line 125, and Q1, which names 'Will' when Capulet directs the 1st Servant to 'Call Peter'. These slips indicate that the role was created by Will Kemp, celebrated for his ability to improvise comedy combining verbal and physical humor as he engaged in direct repartee with the audience. Perhaps, then, in the last part of this scene, Peter baited the musicians before asking 'Why "music with her silver sound"?' Some scholars argue that his humor served as a safety valve to release the tensions created by the contrast between the mourning of those onstage and our knowledge that Juliet is alive.

The final choice in this scene is what to do about the bed. In the original production it may have been pulled back through the central opening, so that Juliet could reappear when the bier appeared in the last scene. Certainly the movement from bed to bier is central to the last arc of the play as the last two places where the lovers are together.

ACT 5

Wednesday midday to Thursday sunrise

Act 5, scene 1: Day 4, Wednesday morning

1–11 'If I may trust the flattering truth of sleep'   Romeo appears in Mantua, alone yet elated (ll. 1–5). For a second time, he has had what he believes to be a prophetic dream and, with no Mercutio to interrupt him or suggest his dream comes from Queen Mab, he can recount his experience (ll. 6–9). While Romeo will soon believe his dream is shockingly inaccurate, we will come to realize it is uncannily prophetic. His first dream predicts disaster if he goes to the Capulet feast yet when he goes he falls in love with Juliet – but his presence prompts Tybalt to issue what proves to be a lethal challenge. His second dream predicts that his wife will resurrect him with kisses, but in a minute he will learn that she is dead and shortly thereafter he will die kissing the wife whose revival follows – creating the bitter irony that '[h]is dream might have told him to kiss *her*, lying apparently dead, until she awakened' (Kliman and Magnus, p. 106).

12–33 'Then I deny/defy you stars'   With the entrance of Balthazar, Romeo's elation may well be expressed physically in how he greets his servant, and first-time spectators may share his hope since the Friar's plan has succeeded so far. When Balthazar explains that Juliet is dead (ll. 17–19), only we can grasp that 'Her body sleeps in Capels' monument' (18) is not a figure of speech but literal truth.

He provokes Romeo's 'Then I deny you stars!' In choosing 'deny', Levenson follows Q2, but many readers and spectators will know this line as 'Then I defy you, stars' because the substantial majority of editors, even if they use nothing else from Q1, make this emendation. Both versions of this speech present Romeo as one who, in contrast with Juliet's parents, the Nurse, and Paris, refuses to accept her death. To *deny* the stars is to negate the claim that they shape human existence, and for Romeo denying the stars makes good sense because the idea that they have produced the death of Juliet suggests that whatever power they embody is, at best, indifferent to human virtue and happiness, and, at worst, actively hostile. To *defy* the stars seems to accept that they shape human destiny but to claim their power is not absolute. Certainly Romeo acts as if he believes there is one decision he can make that the stars cannot influence, namely to end his life at a place and time of his own choosing. Of course, even when he performs this act he does not disprove that the stars control destiny, especially since he acts under a misapprehension which can prompt suspicion that the stars may have determined the suicide he takes as proof of his free will – in which case they will seem malignant indeed.

34–56 'Well, Juliet, I will lie with thee tonight' Whether he speaks of denying or defying the stars, Romeo expresses an overwhelming *im*patience which produces an irresistible need to act and prompts him to recall the Apothecary whose poverty might make him willing to sell poison. If the actor seeks to project a Romeo who matures during the action, then signs of such a change will appear here and in the last scene: 'Notably he has a new concern for others: he feels for the Apothecary as a human being . . . ; he arranges for a letter to his parents; he takes thought for his servant Balthazar; and he feels for the plight of young Paris' (Spencer, 1967, p. 24). Certainly one sign is the quiet, relatively contained way he speaks about suicide compared with the extravagant performance in the Friar's cell.

57–86 'The world is not thy friend, nor the world's law' As he seeks to persuade the Apothecary to violate the law which forbids selling poison, Romeo, perhaps prompted by his experience of being an outlaw, displays not just sympathy but empathy: he sees not only the man's suffering but the cause(s) of that suffering (ll. 58–74). When Romeo notes that 'Famine is in thy cheeks' (l. 69) it would be an act of surprising intimacy if Romeo touched the Apothecary's cheek. As is true with many small roles in Shakespeare, the Apothecary has interesting choices. Is his protest a formality and selling poison really just business as usual? Does he, as the Nurse may do, protest he cannot take Romeo's money but then eagerly seize it? Or does he show genuine reluctance, so that Romeo must really work to overcome his resistance? Is he indifferent to how the poison will be used, or does he show qualms about contributing to the death of another human being? Does he show that he suspects Romeo means to use the poison on himself? If so, how does he look at Romeo? With pity? With horror? Critics have noted that the Apothecary functions as a counterpart to the Friar insofar as both men concoct medicines that can save or kill, and Dessen has pointed out that the Friar can double the role of the Apothecary. Such a doubling would underline the parallel between the Friar, who gives Juliet the potion which mimics death, and the Apothecary, who gives Romeo the poison which produces death.

Act 5, scene 2: Day 4, Wednesday, late afternoon

1–22 'Unhappy fortune . . . The letter was not nice but full of charge' This short scene complicates the representation of the interplay between human agency and the stars as Friar John explains why the letter describing Laurence's plan never reached Romeo. The films by Cukor, Zeffirelli, and Luhrmann all show this event as it happens, and thereby underline the prominent role accident plays in the catastrophe.

23–29 'that Romeo/Hath had no notice of these accidents' The Friar will display great agitation when he speaks of 'these accidents' (l. 26), and the greater his agitation the more he focuses attention on the pattern which already threatens to produce a tragic realization in the final scene. 'The verbal emphasis is frequently on fate; but the logic of the play seems to be rather more than we should like on chance. . . . Perhaps (since we cannot live ourselves back into a belief in the stars) we understand the play better if we think of it as a tragedy of "bad luck" ' (Spencer, pp. 21, 22). The dramatist's shaping of our expectations is complex: while the Friar hastens to the tomb because he fears that Romeo will *not* be there when Juliet wakes, we already know that Romeo *will* be there – not to rescue Juliet but to join her in death. Thus we will anticipate that timing will be everything in the final scene. Yet there is something that, as Levenson notes, original audiences could *not* anticipate, namely that in another of his striking innovations Shakespeare has Paris present at the tomb as well (2000, p. 337).

Act 5, scene 3: Day 4 to Day 5, Wednesday midnight to Thursday dawn

While the scene is clearly situated in a graveyard, the designer and director can, among other options, construct a vault, a freestanding tomb, a bier, or a grave – but they can also use something as simple as a slightly raised flat surface. The design determines whether Romeo actually breaks into something or mimes forcing open a structure, and whether he needs to move Juliet's body, as will happen if she is buried in a trap. The central issue for the director, designer, and actors will be the trade-offs between verisimilitude and visual clarity: does the director place more emphasis on having the audience witness everything or on having the scene conform to the words?

1–21 'Sweet flower, with flowers thy bridal bed I strew' As Paris and his Page enter, the torch indicates that the scene is at night and outdoors, and if there is a visible tomb we will know the scene's location. Otherwise, we learn we are in the graveyard a few lines into Paris's speech. Paris's command to his Page to put out the torch (l. 2) means that the scene unfolds either in imagined or real darkness. Paris orders the Page to step aside – presumably to the edge of the stage or behind a pillar in the original productions – to lie down so he can listen for footsteps (emphasizing how darkness limits visibility), and to whistle if anyone approaches (emphasizing how sound becomes more significant when sight is limited). In his mourning (ll. 12–17), Paris creates a sestet, using the form which can end a sonnet, and is, therefore, appropriate declaring his love. But it will be how he performs his rite that shapes how much we sympathize with his grief.

21–73 'Then have at thee, boy!' Romeo and Balthazar may be carrying some or all the implements specified in their dialogue and the Q1 direction: '*Enter Romeo and Balthasar, with a torch, a mattocke,*

and a crow of yron' (I4^v). After giving Balthazar a letter to his father,
Romeo offers an explanation which implies he will go on living
(ll. 28–32) and warns that he will dismember his servant if he does not
leave (l. 35).This harsh threat recalls his savage speech after the death
of Mercutio, but Romeo balances this savagery by giving Balthazar
money and, as with the Apothecary, wishing him well (l. 42). Still
a keen observer, Balthazar notes Romeo's wild aspect (l. 44) and
hides rather than leaves. The stage is thus primed with four people
operating in imagined darkness.

In calling attention to Romeo's wild appearance Balthazar
prompts us to try to read Romeo ourselves. Is he in an exalted state,
convinced that he will indeed be reunited in death with Juliet or is he
in despair at being separated from her? Or is he oscillating between
extremes? Especially if he must actually attack a structure holding
Juliet, how he does so may offer one indication of his state at this
moment. When Paris – who, like Tybalt, identifies Romeo by his
voice – steps forward to halt this 'unhallowed toil' (l. 54), Romeo's
speeches show he is precariously balanced between gentle and savage
elements. The gentle element is foremost as he tries to dissuade this
man he does not recognize from apprehending him (ll. 62–3), and
hints he has come to kill himself (ll. 64–7). When Paris persists, however, Romeo cries 'Then have at thee, boy!' (l. 70), echoing Tybalt
(3.1.65, 130). Equating Romeo with Tybalt is a daring move that risks
subverting his stature as a tragic hero, and has troubled critics and
directors alike: '[t]he slaughtering of Paris is wanton and serves little
dramatic purpose' (Granville-Barker, p. 312). However, Hibbard suggests that the moment when Romeo kills Paris is the play's turning
point since '[i]t is not until Romeo kills Paris . . . that all hope and
possibility of a fortunate conclusion finally disappear, and the sense
of inevitability, so characteristic of tragedy, at last makes itself fully
felt' (1981, pp. 121, 122). Moreover, if the fight compels us to recognize
that Romeo has momentarily become like Tybalt, it thereby also compels us to recognize that this transformation results from the way the
feud coerces Romeo into adopting a reductive definition of manhood.
What Snyder says about Juliet is 3.2 applies to us: now *we* must superimpose Romeo the killer on Romeo the lover and, like Juliet, we may
resist doing so. Directors who eliminate Paris from this scene simplify
the relation between hate and love, hence simplify the interpretive
challenges that the audience must confront.

In this fight, a key choice concerns the weapon(s) Romeo uses. Since the Friar soon discovers 'these masterless and gory swords' (l. 142), the text seems to direct both men to use their rapiers. At the moment Paris confronts him, however, Romeo is still opening the tomb (l. 73), so one option is for him to use the tool that is in his hand. In the eighteenth century, both David Garrick and Spranger Barry used the crowbar and their gesture as they raised it over their heads was both famous and mocked, since Romeo was using an ungentlemanly weapon and since this pause seemed to provide Paris time to run him through with his sword (see the discussion of Garrick's version in Key Productions). But using an ungentlemanly weapon can serve as further evidence of Romeo's transformation. Romeo can, of course, drop the crowbar to draw his rapier. Or he can be forced to kill a highly aggressive Paris, using Paris's own weapon (which may necessitate modifying the Friar's speech).

74–87 'Death, lie thou there, by a dead man interred' Romeo's long soliloquy (ll. 74–120) and Juliet's short final solo (ll. 160–70) serve as the last of the distinctive arias by the lovers before the play shifts to the less exalted speech in which the survivors try to make sense of the catastrophe. One crucial feature is the way Romeo uses direct address to create a virtual dialogue with the corpses of Paris, Tybalt, and Juliet. What appears to be a simple oscillation proves to be a tightening gyre in which he recapitulates the plot, creates suspense, and realizes the *liebestod* motif.

As his fury ebbs, Romeo kneels and may use the torch to learn the identity of the man he has killed. He remembers that Paris 'should have married Juliet' (l. 78), but rather than enraging him, as we might expect, the fact that Paris loved Juliet enough to die for her prompts Romeo to address him as his brother in misfortune (l. 82), and to promise a respectful burial (l. 83). As he moves Paris to or into the tomb, his perception of how Juliet's presence illuminates the space (ll. 85–6) echoes the words he spoke when he first saw her (1.4.157). Moreover, Romeo moves from empathy to identity as he looks at the body of Paris and sees himself as one who is just minutes away from becoming a corpse. It is striking, moreover, that while he rarely directly addresses his lady as 'Juliet' in their scenes together, now he repeats her name like an incantation, as if urgent repetition might conjure her back from the dead. He thus echoes the times when Benvolio, Mercutio, and Juliet repeated his name as a form of conjuration.

88–96 'And death's pale flag is not advanced there'   One of Shakespeare's most consistent dramaturgic devices is the use of repetition-with-a-difference and in *Romeo and Juliet* part of what makes the last scene so powerful is the contrast between Romeo's earlier attempt and his present suicide. Whereas the first attempt comes when his despair brings Romeo to the brink of madness, in this scene, following the fury of his encounter with Paris, Romeo moves steadily toward his objective, and verbally, a least, seems to do so in a state of peculiar elation. Whereas in the earlier scene success would have meant abandoning Juliet, in this scene his aim is to rejoin her – although it is another bitter irony that his success leaves Juliet abandoned when the potion wears off. Romeo tacitly calls attention to this contrast when he probes his 'light'ning before death' (l. 90): how can he be so exhilarated when he has just killed a man, is looking at the corpse of his wife, and is preparing to kill himself? When he turns his attention to Juliet, his perception of her life-like appearance may either increase his commitment to suicide or give him pause, as if he is puzzled by the signs of life but has no idea what to make of them. Whatever his response, the moment produces excruciating suspense, in which our knowledge that Juliet is alive becomes a source of hope and despair as well as a reminder of our impotence. Shakespeare typically produces this effect at moments balancing life and death as when Hamlet examines the foils, Gertrude prepares to drink from the poisoned cup, Edmund announces his desire to do 'some good' yet delays revealing his order to execute Cordelia, and the courtiers in *The Winter's Tale* kneel to save Hermione's newborn daughter. In these moments, Shakespeare designs the action so as to both arouse and frustrate our impulse to intervene. When these moments work – they are especially effective in small theaters with thrust stages – their power is registered by the fact that you have to *resist* the impulse to move. Here, the impulse to intervene is verbal, so that when Romeo notes that Juliet's lips and cheeks are still red (ll. 94–5), we want to shout 'That's because she's still alive!' Soon, however, as he reaches for the poison, we may need to suppress a powerful physical impulse to leap onstage to restrain him.

97–101 'Forgive me, cousin'   Romeo comes close to replicating Juliet's action in 4.3 when she addressed the vision of her cousin, but he is not so much hallucinating as ventriloquizing a dialogue. Does he address this plea to a corpse he and we can see? Or does he in effect create that corpse by his address? The important point is not whether the corpse is present but rather the way Romeo calls attention to Tybalt's role in unleashing the destructive power of the feud and the way the interplay of hate and love has trapped Romeo and Juliet. And what tone of voice does he use and what gestures does he make as he asks for pardon?

101–120 'Here's to my love!'   When Romeo turns back to Juliet he returns to the image of Death and the Maiden. But where Capulet sees death as a rival who will inherit all, Romeo, having just dispatched one rival, believes he can triumph over the other by dispatching himself. Through the rising energy of his virtual dialogue, Romeo, like Juliet as she prepares to drink the potion, achieves the escape velocity he needs to commit suicide (ll. 111–12). Does the actor take a last look at Juliet to absorb the beauty that first enchanted him? Does he perform a last embrace, reanimating their first touch, their hands joined in marriage, and their night together? Does he seek a last kiss, echoing their parting kiss two days earlier? When he addresses the poison does his address echo Juliet's toast to Romeo? His speech (ll. 119–20) acknowledges that the poison is as swift as promised, but also that it is 'quick' because it frees him to enter a new life with Juliet. Romeo ends by repeating the complimentary pun, proclaiming 'Thus with a kiss I die' (l. 120). Does he die upon a kiss or is the poison so fast-acting that it prevents him from achieving this consummation? When Romeo succeeds, the kiss provides a resonant closure; but it is possible that 'Thy drugs are quick' registers his discovery that he will die before he can perform that kiss, in which case we confront a painful dissonance that may thwart our hunger for at least hint of a reunion.

121–147 'Romeo, O, pale! Who else? What, Paris too?'   Like Romeo, the Friar may enter with a crowbar, as well as a spade and a lantern, which becomes the second light on stage. The issue of timing is emphasized when he describes himself as stumbling in haste (l. 122), and may well indicate the Friar's agitated state as a prelude to his being overcome by fear. 'Who's there?' registers the darkness, and he may use his lantern to see Balthazar's face (ll. 122, 123). Only after asking about the torch that 'burneth in the Capel's monument' (ll. 125–7) does he learn the shocking news that Romeo has been in the tomb for some time (l. 130). In addition, his admission that 'Fear comes upon me' (l. 135) must be heightened when Balthazar recounts his dream that Romeo fought with and killed another man. Q1 supplies another direction incorporated by many editors: '*Fryer stoops and lookes on the blood and weapons*' (K2ʳ; ll. 140–3). If in the first scene Romeo's 'Ay me, what fray was here?' (1.1.169) is prompted by bloody weapons on the ground, the Friar's action here can connect the first and last scenes. In the tomb, the bodies prompt him to speak of 'this lamentable chance' (ll. 145–6), so that once again his speech and action will emphasize the powerful role that accident plays in the catastrophe.

148–159 'Thy husband in thy bosom there lies dead'   When he sees Juliet move, (l. 147), the Friar realizes that she is waking, but she may have started to do so before he notices, before Romeo is dead, or even before he has drunk the poison – and every one of these options will, of course, increase the pain for us. Facing the horror of Romeo's death, it must be a relief to the Friar that part of his plan has worked, but devastating when Juliet asks 'Where is my Romeo?' (l. 150). He is so unnerved by the noise of the Watch that he tactlessly announces 'Thy husband in thy bosom there lies dead' (l. 155), and it is up to the actress how Juliet registers the shock while she also rejects or ignores his five commands to 'Come' as panic makes him flee.

160–170 'O happy dagger,/This is thy sheath. There rust, and let me die'   It is a striking pattern, which can be emphasized by the placement of the bier, that we see Juliet waking up at the end of the third act, not waking up at the end of the fourth act, and now waking up at the climax of the fifth act. That is, we share the dawn of the last three days of her life, as we also share the dawn with Romeo on two days. Here, Juliet quickly makes her last two choices: in a single sentence she decides not to follow the Friar to safety (l. 160), and although her words are not as harsh as her earlier 'Ancient damnation!' they mark the moment when she cuts herself off from the last living person she trusted. Since her only connection is with Romeo, it makes sense that she resolves to rejoin him in death (ll. 160–70). When she finds the cup in his hand, does she raise it to her lips to confirm that it is empty? She kisses him and acknowledges 'Thy lips are warm' (l. 167), detecting a sign of ebbing life – a mirror image of Romeo detecting yet not knowing what to make of the signs of rising life in Juliet. As the noise warns her she is about to be discovered, she seizes Romeo's dagger and, echoing his address to the poison, stabs herself. The fact that both lovers expire with 'dies' on their lips, using the word that meant both to expire and to achieve orgasm, indicates that this double suicide is their way of achieving love-in-death. Many productions in the nineteenth century and the first part of the twentieth century ended here (Levenson, 2000, p. 349; Loehlin, 2002, p. 245).

171–207 'Search, seek, and know how this foul murder comes'
The third entrance of the Prince parallels a pattern that Shakespeare later deployed in *Hamlet*, where the court assembles at the beginning, middle, and end of the action. Here, the Prince's return registers the fact that, despite his ultimatum in 1.1 and his decision to exile Romeo in 3.1, he has failed to stem the tide of violence. This time, however, lacking Benvolio to explain what happened, the Prince himself must investigate the events that have produced this bloody outcome (l. 158) – including, as the Watch notes, the puzzling second death of a woman who apparently died a day earlier.

208–215 'Come, Montague, for thou art early up' When Montague enters and announces that Romeo's banishment has killed Lady Montague (ll. 210–1), it is a performance choice whether he is simply expressing his grief or also accusing the Prince of precipitating her death. When the Prince banished Romeo, did her response foreshadow her death? Is Lady Montague so old that her death comes as little surprise? Or is she young, so that the feud proves able to kill a woman in the prime of life? In Q1 Montague adds that 'yong *Benuolio* is deceased too' (K3^r), so that the entire next generation dies in the course of the action. Productions that include this speech present Montague as someone who has lost his wife, his son, and his nephew.

216–85 'Romeo, there dead, was husband to that Juliet' The Friar's 41-line retrospective exposition has often been criticized for the fact that, however much the characters need to learn what has happened, the audience already knows the facts he recounts – and indeed knows more than he knows. Yet as Bertrand Evans has pointed out (1979, pp. 50–1), as the Friar speaks the survivors must confront the ways in which their decisions contributed to the destruction of the lovers (ll. 231–9). How does the Prince respond when he realizes that in banishing Romeo he contributed not only to the deaths of the lovers but of his kinsman Paris? How does Capulet react when he realizes that by insisting that Juliet marry Paris he drove her to use the potion which produced her apparent death and prompted Romeo to commit suicide? How does Balthazar react when he realizes that by informing Romeo that Juliet was dead he inadvertently contributed to the death of the master he was attempting to serve, as well as that master's wife? How does Montague respond to this series of revelations about the life and death of the son whose condition seemed so desperate in the first place? How does the Prince respond to learning the cost imposed by his failure to suppress the feud? How harsh is he in rebuking Capulet and Montague? Is he at all reluctant to declare the Friar innocent? How do the fathers respond? Does each attempt to blame the other? When he realizes it is Romeo's dagger in Juliet's corpse does Capulet try to attack Montague? Does Montague respond in kind? Does it seem as if the whole cycle will start again?

286–304 'See what a scourge is laid upon your hate'   In his speech concluding 'All are punished' (ll. 291–5), the Prince offers what sounds like a sentence that can never be overturned because no appeal is possible. When he notes that he has 'lost a brace of kinsmen', he recalls the full roster of those killed: Tybalt and Juliet, Romeo and Lady Montague (and, in Q1, Benvolio), and Mercutio and Paris. Whether we imagine the scourge as an implement wielded by fortune, fate, or providence, the symmetry of the deaths seems to gesture toward some more encompassing tragic pattern. His words also prompt the fathers to end the feud, and until recently a sincere reconciliation is what performances offered and what audiences seemed to desire. It is possible, however, to perform the scene so as to undercut the reconciliation – so that, for example, when Montague says 'But I can give more' (l. 298) he is being competitive, not generous, emphasizing that he possesses the wealth necessary to 'raise her statue in pure gold' (l. 299) and compelling Capulet to meet his challenge. Even without such overtly subversive actions, however, the idea of the golden statues can '[resonate] disturbingly with Romeo's recent diatribe against gold as poison' (Snyder, 1996, p. 96). On the other hand, '[i]n a final touch of pathos, [the] fathers tender belated offers of dower and dowry over the bodies of two dead children':

> With equal offers and clasped hands, the parents enact the spousal agreement between families that should have preceded the marriage of the young lovers, were it not for the feud. As the momentarily widowed wife of Romeo, Juliet will have from the Montagues a golden jointure equal to the golden dowry she brings from the Capulets.   (Cook, p. 210)

Insofar as the fathers can be seen as completing the marriage, they can also be seen as ratifying the principle for which their children lived and died: '[i]n its treatment of romantic love and of marriage based on free choice by lovers, *Romeo and Juliet* has been a more fully and influentially political work than has usually been recognised' (Watts, 1991, p. xii).

305–10 'A glooming peace this morning with it brings'

Although Shakespeare does not have the Chorus return after its second appearance, the Prince's speech can function like a final chorus both in asserting that 'never was a story of more woe/Than this of Juliet and her Romeo' (ll. 309–10) and in urging those on stage and those in the audience to continue a reflective conversation (l. 307).

Exeunt omnes: 'tragedy's chronic problem of removing the bodies'

In the theater the ending of a Shakespeare tragedy always raises the question of how to stage the '*Exeunt omnes*', and how this was handled by Shakespeare's company has been discussed earlier (see Chapter 1). As with the other pivotal scenes, the solution in a modern production will depend in part on the nature of the stage and the setting. The range of solutions is wide, and includes exits where the bodies remain, but also quite elaborate endings in which the statues appear on stage – which can be accomplished simply by having the lovers rise and move in ways that indicate they are now sculptured objects. Such a staging can reinforce the solemnity of the moment and emphasize how one good outcome emerges from the destruction of the younger generation. But as with the ending of Michael Bogdanov's 1986 RSC production it is possible to stage this scene as a cynical public relations event, meant to hide the bankruptcy of a murderous power structure (see Chapter 4).

Finally, how does this assembly of survivors leave the stage? If, for example, the Capulets leave by one door and the Montagues by the other, they suggest that they may have ended the feud but not yet developed the harmony necessary to insure that it is buried with the bodies and renounced with the statues. Another possibility, as Gurr suggests, would be to create a sense of emerging harmony by having the families exit together through a large central door (1996, p. 25).

In the play's concluding words, the Prince offers a cue for both the families and the spectators to reflect on the events in order to develop a more comprehensive, more nuanced understanding. As we exit, we too might hope to 'Go hence to have more talk of these sad things' (l. 307). We keep attending performances of plays such as *Romeo and Juliet* because we are drawn by the possibility that the next performance may realize potentials we have never perceived, provoke new insights, and prompt us to articulate a more precise understanding of this tragedy. We keep reading and imagining performances both for the discoveries such an engagement makes possible and for the ways in which such imaginary performances can sharpen our perception of actual productions.

3 The Play's Source and Cultural Context

The items in this chapter include excerpts from the source for Shakespeare's play; documents on the honor code and violence; and poems in the forms that Shakespeare used in the play, including two sonnets, part of an epithalamium, and an *aubade*.

Arthur Brooke's *The Tragicall Historye of Romeus and Juliet* (1562)

Shakespeare's primary source was *The Tragicall Historye of Romeus and Juliet*, a narrative poem by Arthur Brooke (died 1563), which was published in 1562 and reprinted in 1582 and 1587. Four versions of the story preceded Brooke's, and these versions are available in translation in Nicole Prunster's *Romeo and Juliet before Shakespeare: Four Early Stories of Star-Crossed Love* (2000). The crucial versions were the second and the fourth. The second version was by Luigi da Porto, and appeared in *Istoria novellamente ritrovata de due Nobili Amanti* (written in 1524, published c. 1530, and reprinted in 1535 and 1539). As Levenson has demonstrated, this was the most important version because da Porto 'established a sequence of twelve incidents which would remain fundamentally unchanged through the sixteenth century' (2000, p. 5). The fourth version was a French adaptation by Pierre Boaistuau, published in a volume entitled *Histoires Tragiques extraictes des Oeuvres italiens de Bandel* (1559). This version was translated into English prose by William Painter, and it appeared in volume two of his *Painter's Palace of Pleasure* (1567). Scholars agree that Brooke based his version on Boaistuau.

Brooke's 3020-line poem is written in poulter's measure – alternate lines of 12 and 14 syllables, with six stresses in the first and seven stresses in the second line. Shakespeare transformed Brooke's narrative in terms of plot, character, and language, and reduced the narrative voice to the two appearances of the Chorus. In terms of the plot, his most important decision was to reduce this nine-month narrative to an action unfolding in a little more than four days, as well as recalibrating the ratio of choice and accident that produces the tragic outcome. The selections enable readers to analyze some of Shakespeare's transformations. They begin with an excerpt from Brooke's preface 'To the Reader', which offers a moralistic interpretation of the story and an anti-Catholic perspective on the Friar – although the poem itself is more sympathetic to the lovers and less harsh on the Friar. This is followed by the 'Argument', a synopsis written as a sonnet, which may have suggested the form Shakespeare used for the speeches of the Chorus. The excerpts from the poem come from the scene at the Capulet feast where Juliet is seated between Romeus and Mercutio (ll. 251–90); the scene in the Friar's cell where Romeus learns that the Prince has banished him for killing Tybalt (ll. 1343–60); the scene in which Romeus and Juliet confront their separation (ll. 1701–28); and the final speeches of Romeus (2627–88) and Juliet (2765–92). From *The Tragicall Historye of Romeus and Juliet* by Arthur Brooke, printed by Richard Tottell in 1562. I have modernized the spelling and punctuation in these extracts. The line numbers correspond with those reprinted in volume 1 of Geoffrey Bullough's *Narrative and Dramatic Sources of Shakespeare* (1957), pp. 284–363.

From 'To The Reader'

And as each flower yieldeth honey to the bee, so every example ministreth good lessons, to the well disposed mind. The glorious triumph of the continent man upon the lusts of wanton flesh encourageth men to honest restraint of wild affections; the shameful and wretched ends of such as have yielded their liberty thrall to foul desires, teach men to withhold themselves from the headlong fall of loose dishonesty. So, to like effect, by sundry means, the good man's example biddeth men to be good, and the evil man's mischief warneth men not to be evil. To this good end serve all ill ends of ill beginnings. And to this end (good Reader) is this tragical matter written, to describe unto thee a couple of unfortunate lovers, thralling themselves to unhonest desire, neglecting the authority and advice of parents and friends, conferring their principal counsels with drunken gossips, and superstitious friars (the naturally fit instruments of unchastity), attempting all adventures of peril for the attaining of their wished lust, using auricular confession (the key of whoredom and treason) for furtherance of their purpose, abusing the honorable name of lawful marriage to cloak the shame of stolen contracts; finally, by all means of unhonest life, hasting to most unhappy death. . . . Though I saw the same argument lately set forth on stage with more commendation then I can look for (being there much better set forth then I have or can do) yet the same matter penned as it is, may serve to like good effect, if the readers do bring with them like minds, to consider it. Which hath the more encouraged me to publish it, such as it is. Ar. Br.

The Argument

Love hath inflamed twain by sudden sight.
    And both do grant the thing that both desire.
    They wed in shrift by counsel of a friar.
    Young Romeus climbs fair Juliet's bower by night.
Three months he doth enjoy his chief delight.
    By Tybalt's rage, provoked unto ire,
    He payeth death to Tybalt for his hire.
    A banished man, he scapes by secret flight.
New marriage is offered to his wife.
    She drinks a drink that seems to reeve her breath.
    They bury her, that sleeping yet hath life.
Her husband hears the tidings of her death.
    He drinks his bane. And she with Romeus' knife,
    When she awakes, her self (alas) she slayeth.

Romeus, Juliet, and Mercutio at the Capulet party (ll. 251–290)

Fair Juliet turned to her chair with pleasant cheer
And glad she was her Romeus approached was so near.
At th'one side of her chair, her lover Romeo,
And on the other side there sat one called Mercutio,
A courtier that each where was highly had in price,
For he was courteous of his speech, and pleasant of device
Even as a Lion would among the lambs be bold,
Such was among the bashfull maids, Mercutio to behold.
With friendly gripe he seized fair Juliet's snowish hand.

A gift he had that nature gave him in his swathing band,   260
That frozen mountain ice was never half so cold
As were his hands, though ne'er so near the fire he did them hold.
As soon as had the knight the virgin's right hand raught
Within his trembling hand her left hath loving Romeus caught.
For he wist well himself for her abode most pain;
And well he wist she loved him best, unless she list to fain.
Then she with tender hand his tender palm hath prest:
What joy trow you was graffed so in Romeus cloven breast?
The sudden sweet delight hath stopped quite his tongue
Ne can he claim of her his right, ne crave redress of wrong.   270
But she espied straight way, by changing of his hue
From pale to red, from red to pale, and so from pale anew,
That vehement love was cause, why so his tongue did stay
And so much more she longed to hear what love could teach him say.
When she had longed long, and he long held his peace,
And her desire of hearing him by silence did increase,
At last with trembling voice and shamefast cheer, the maid
Unto her Romeus turned her self, and thus to him she said.
O blessed be the time of thy arrival here:
But ere she could speak forth the rest, to her love drew so near   280
And so within her mouth, her tongue he glued fast,
That no word could scape her more, than what already past.
In great contented ease the young man straight is rapt,
What chance (quoth he) unware to me O lady mine is hapt?
That gives you worthy cause, my coming here to bliss?
Fair Juliet was come again unto her self by this.
First ruthfully she looked, then said with smiling cheer
Marvel no whit my heart's delight, my only knight and fere
Mercutio's icy hand had all to frozen mine
And of thy goodness thou again hast warmed it with thine.   290

Romeus in the Friar's cell (ll. 1343–1360)

On Fortune eke he railed, he called her deaf, and blind,
Unconstant, fond, deceitfull, rash, unruthful, and unkind
And to him self he laid a great part of the fault,
For that he slew, and was not slain, in fighting with Tybalt.
He blamed all the world, and all he did defy
But Juliet, for whom he lived, for whom eke would he die.
When after raging fits, appeased was his rage,
And when his passions (poured forth) gan partly to assuage,   1350

So wisely did the friar unto his tale reply,
That he straight cared for his life, that erst had care to die.
Art thou, quoth he, a man? thy shape saith so thou art:
Thy crying and thy weeping eyes, denote a woman's heart,
For manly reason is quite from of thy mind outchased,
And in her stead affections lewd, and fancies highly placed,
So that I stood in doubt this hour (at the least)
If thou a man, or woman wert, or else a brutish beast.
A wise man in the midst of troubles and distress,
Still stands not wailing present harm, but seeks his harm's redress . . .

1360

Romeus and Juliet confront sunrise (1701–1728)

Thus these two lovers pass away the weary night,
In pain and plaint, not (as they wont) in pleasure and delight.
But now (somewhat too soon) in farthest East arose
Fair Lucifer, the golden star that Lady Venus chose,
Whose course appointed is, with speedy race to run,
A messenger of dawning day, and of the rising sun.
Then fresh Aurora, with her pale and silver glade,
Did clear the skies, and from the earth, had chased ugly shade.
When thou ne lookest wide, ne closely dost thou wink,
When Phoebus from our hemisphere, in western wave doth sink.   1710
What color then the heavens do shew unto thine eyes,
The same (or like) saw Romeus in farthest Eastern skies.
As yet, he saw no day, ne could he call it night,
With equal force, decreasing dark, fought with increasing light.
Then Romeus in arms his lady gan to fold,
With friendly kiss, and ruthfully she gan her knight behold.
With solemn oath they both their sorrowful leave do take;
They swear no stormy troubles shall their steady friendship shake.
Then careful Romeus, again to cell returns,
And in her chamber secretly our joyless Juliet mourns.   1720
Now hugey clouds of care, of sorrow and of dread,
The clearness of their gladsome hearts hath wholly overspread.
When golden crested Phoebus boosteth him in sky,
And under earth, to scape revenge, his deadly foe doth fly,
Then hath these lovers' day an end, their night begun,
For each of them to other is, as to the world the sun.
The dawning they shall see, ne summer any more,
But blackfaced night with winter rough (ah) beaten over sore.

Romeus's suicide (2627–2688)

Now Peter, that knew not the purpose of his heart,
Obediently a little way withdrew himself apart,
And then our Romeus (the vault stone set upright)
Descended down, and in his hand he bear the candle light.   2630
And then with piteous eye, the body of his wife
He gan behold, who surely was the organ of his life.
For whom unhappy now he is, but erst was blist.
He watered her with tears, and then an hundred times her kist,
And in his folded arms, full straightly he her plight,
But no way could his greedy eyes be filled with her sight.
His fearfull hands he laid upon her stomach cold,
And them on divers parts beside, the woeful wight did hold.
But when he could not find the signs of life he sought,
Out of his cursed box he drew the poison that he bought.   2640
Whereof he greedily devoured the greater part,
And then he cried with deadly sigh, fetched from his mourning heart:
O Juliet, of whom the world unworthy was,
From which, for world's unworthiness thy worthy ghost did pass,
What death more pleasant could my heart wish to abide,
Then that which here it suffreth now, so near thy friendly side?
Or else so glorious tomb, how could my youth have craved,
As in one self-same vault with thee haply to be ingraved?
What Epitaph more worth, or half so excellent,
To consecrate my memory, could any man invent,   2650
As this, our mutual and our piteous sacrifice
Of life, set light for love. But while he talketh in this wise,
And thought as yet a while his dolors to enforce,
His tender heart began to faint, pressed with the venom's force,
Which little and little gan to overcome his heart,
And whilst his busy eyne he threw about to every part,
He saw hard by the corce of sleeping Juliet,
Bold Tybalt's carcass dead, which was not all consumed yet.
To whom (as having life) in this sort speaketh he:
Ah cousin dear Tybalt, whereso thy restless sprite now be,   2660
With stretched hands to thee for mercy now I cry,
For that before thy kindly hour I forced thee to die.
But if with quenched life, not quenched be thine ire,
But with revenging lust as yet thy heart be set on fire,
What more amends, or cruel wreak desirest thou
To see on me, then this which here is shewed forth to thee now?
Who reft by force of arms from thee thy living breath,

The same with his own hand (thou seest) doth poison himself to death.
And for he caused thee in tomb too soon to lie,
Too soon also, younger than thou, himself he layeth by.   2670
These said, when he gan feel the poison's force prevail,
And little and little mastered life, for aye began to fail,
Kneeling upon his knees, he said with voice full low.
Lord Christ, that so to ransom me descendedst long ago
Out of thy father's bosom, and in the virgin's womb
Didst put on flesh, Oh let my plaint out of this hollow tomb,
Pierce through the air, and grant my suit may favour find;
Take pity on my sinful and my poor afflicted mind.
For well enough I know, this body is but clay,
Nought but a mass of sin, too frail, and subject to decay.   2680
Then pressed with extreme grief, he threw with so great force,
His overpressed parts upon his lady's wailed corpse,
That now his weakened heart, weakened with torments past,
Unable to abide this pang, the sharpest and the last,
Remained quite deprived, of sense and kindly strength,
And so the long imprisoned soul hath freedom won at length.
Ah cruel death, too soon, too soon was this divorce,
Twixt youthful Romeus' heavenly sprite, and his fair earthy corpse.

Juliet's suicide (2765–2792)

When Juliet saw her self left in the vault alone,
That freely she might work her will, for let or stay was none,
Then once for all, she took the cause of all her harms,
The body dead of Romeus, and clasped it in her arms.
Then she with earnest kiss, sufficiently did prove,
That more than by the fear of death she was attaint by love.   2770
And then past deadly fear, for life ne had she care,
With hasty hand she did draw out the dagger that he ware.
O welcome death (quoth she) end of unhappiness,
That also art beginning of assured happiness:
Fear not to dart me now, thy stripe no longer stay,
Prolong no longer now my life, I hate this long delay,
For straight my parting sprite, out of this carcass fled,
At ease shall find my Romeus' sprite, among so many dead.
And thou my loving lord, Romeus my trusty feer,
If knowledge yet do rest in thee, if thou these words dost hear   2780
Receive thou her whom thou didst love so lawfully,

That caused (alas) thy violent death although unwillingly;
And therefore willingly offers to thee her ghost,
To th'end that no wight else but thou, might have just cause to boast
Th'enjoying of my love, which ay I have reserved,
Free from the rest, bound unto thee, that hast it well deserved.
That so our parted sprites, from light that we see here,
In place of endless light and bliss, may ever live yfere.
These said, her ruthless hand through-girt her valiant heart.
Ah, Ladies, help with tears to wail the lady's deadly smart.   2790
She groans, she stretcheth out her limbs, she shuts her eyes,
And from her corpse the sprite doth fly. [W]hat should I say? she dies.

Honor, Violence, and Christian Ethics

William Segar, Preface to *The Book of Honor and Armes* (1590)

The code of honor espoused by the English aristocracy and gentry
was problematic not only because it provoked frequent outbursts
of violence, which both Queen Elizabeth and King James sought to
end by a series of proclamations, but because it contradicted the
state-sponsored Christian religion, whether in the Catholic form represented in *Romeo and Juliet* or in the Protestant form embodied in
the Church of England. Honor both depended on and nurtured the
sin of pride; it contradicted the command forbidding murder; and it
prompted people to violate the commands to love one's neighbor, to
turn the other cheek, and to forgive one's enemies. These problems
are registered in the Preface written by Segar. This excerpt, slightly
modernized, comes from the facsimile edited by Diane Bornstein
(1975), pp. A2–A3

> The cause of all quarrel is injury and reproach, but the matter of content
> is justice and honor. . . . True it is, that the Christian law willeth men to
> be of so perfect patience, as not only to endure injurious words, but also
> quietly to suffer every force and violence. Notwithstanding, for so much
> as none (or very few men) have attained such perfection, the laws of all
> nations, for avoiding further inconvinces, and the manifestation of truth,
> have . . . permitted, that such questions as could not be civilly proved by
> confession, witness, or other circumstances, should receive judgment by
> fight and combat, supposing that GOD (who only knoweth the secret
> thoughts of all men) would give victory to him that justly adventured his
> life, for truth, honor and justice.

Seeing then that all humane laws have permitted the trial of arms, and that every injurious action not repulsed, is by common consent of all martiall minds holden a thing dishonorable, infamous, and reproachful; it cannot be, but at some times and occasions such questions and quarrels shall arise, as necessarily must receive trial by the sword. And *Cicero* saith, that he who repulseth not an injury, being able, offendeth no less than if he had abandoned his friends, parents and country. By these reasons appeareth that the trial by arms is not only natural, but also necessary and allowable. Notwithstanding, for that the vulgar sort (and many right noble also) be ignorant what are the true causes requiring trial of arms, and what words or deeds are of such quality as ought be repulsed or revenged; I have at the earnest requests and often desires of very honorable friends ... reduced into this small volume all causes of quarrel or combat, the nature of injuries and repulses, the equality and disequality of men, who may be challenged, and for what respects challenges ought be refused: with many other things in matter of honor and arms worthy to be known and considered. (A2)

'Art thou now come? Then I will have a bout with thee'

While there is no evidence that Shakespeare himself ever engaged in a duel, the playwright and poet Ben Jonson, for example, was branded on his thumb after he killed an actor in a duel and saved himself from hanging by pleading benefit of clergy. But Shakespeare and members of his audiences might well have known of the encounter in which another playwright, Christopher Marlowe, while walking in Hog Lane on 18 September 1590, 'between the second and third hour of the afternoon', was challenged by and began a sword-fight with William Bradley. After first attacking Marlowe, Bradley attacked the poet Thomas Watson when Watson arrived on the scene. This fight suggests how the opening scene of the *Romeo and Juliet* would have reminded some spectators of how violence could erupt on a London street. And it records a fight between three men that bears some resemblance to the fights in 3.1. What follows is from the report from the coroner's inquest as repeated in the document recording Watson's pardon. From Constance Kuriyama's *Christopher Marlowe: A Renaissance Life* (2002, p. 206).

a certain Thomas Watson, late of London, gentleman, arrived on the scene ... upon the noise of the crowd standing there, in order to separate the aforesaid William Bradley and Christopher Morley who were thus

fighting, to preserve our peace. And for this reason he then and there drew
his sword. Whereupon the aforementioned Christopher Morley withdrew
and stopped fighting. And whereupon the aforesaid William Bradley, seeing the same Thomas Watson intervening with his sword drawn spoke
to him in these English words, as follows, 'Art thou now come? Then I
will have a bout with thee.' And immediately the same William Bradley
then and there assaulted the aforementioned Thomas Watson, and, with
sword and dagger of iron and steel, then and there beat, wounded, and
maltreated the same Thomas Watson. So that, despairing of his life, the
aforementioned Thomas Watson then and there defended himself against
the aforesaid William Bradley with his aforesaid sword of iron and steel
of the value of three shillings, four pence, which he then and there had
and held in his right hand, and for the saving of his life he fled from the
aforesaid William Bradley all the way to a certain ditch in the aforesaid
lane to the point where, on peril of his life, he could flee no further. And
the aforesaid William Bradley continuing his attack, the aforementioned
Thomas Watson was then and there newly cut. Therefore the aforesaid
Thomas Watson, for the saving of his life, then and there struck the aforesaid William Bradley with his aforesaid sword a mortal blow or wound
in and on the right side of the chest near the nipple of the same William
Bradley, of the depth of six inches and of the width of one inch, of which
same mortal stroke the same William Bradley, at Finsbury aforesaid in the
aforesaid Middlesex County, instantly died.

Poetic forms in action: sonnet, epithalamium, and aubade

One of the features of *Romeo and Juliet* that would have appealed to
educated members of the original audiences was the use of poetic
forms for dramatic purposes. The obvious example is the use of the
sonnet, which occurs in the two speeches by the Q2 Chorus and in
the dialogue in which Romeo and Juliet first woo each other.

Sonnets

The sonnet was an appropriate form to employ because in the 1590s
the sonnet, whether as a single poem or in a sequence, enabled the
writer or the invented speaker to explore his (or, later, her) relations
with a beloved. Furthermore, since the form was highly conventional, it could be used not only to express but also to contest,
transform, and revise ideas and tropes. For example, in 1.1 Romeo
speaks of his love for Rosaline using the oxymora and antitheses that

were part of Petrarch's legacy. His speeches can be juxtaposed with Shakespeare's sonnet #130. First, the poem mocks the clichés that constitute Romeo's discourse about Rosaline and, like all effective parodies, helps us grasp the content of those clichés. Second, it provides an example of the *blazon,* the pattern Mercutio uses when he offers his satirical anatomy of Rosaline.

130

My mistress' eyes are nothing like the sun;
Coral is far more red than her lips' red;
If snow be white, why then her breasts are dun;
If hairs be wires, black wires grow on her head.
I have seen roses damask'd, red and white,
But no such roses see I in her cheeks,
And in some perfumes is there more delight
Than in the breath that from my mistress reeks.
I love to hear her speak, yet well I know
That music hath a far more pleasing sound;
I grant I never saw a goddess go,
My mistress when she walks treads on the ground.
   And yet, by heaven, I think my love as rare
   As any she belied with false compare.   (*Riverside*, p. 1867)

Sonnet #116, by contrast, offers a statement of love as an absolute value that seems to correspond in some ways with the sense of absolute commitment Romeo and Juliet display in their life and death.

116

Let me not to the marriage of true minds
Admit impediments; love is not love
Which alters when it alteration finds,
Or bends with the remover to remove.
O no, it is an ever-fixed mark
That looks on tempests and is never shaken;
It is the star to every wand'ring bark,
Whose worth's unknown, although his highth be taken.
Love's not Time's fool, though rosy lips and cheeks
Within his bending sickle's compass come,
Love alters not with his brief hours and weeks,
But bears it out even to the edge of doom.

If this be error and upon me proved,
I never writ, nor no man ever loved.   (*Riverside*, p. 1864)

Epithalamium

Some auditors would have recognized that Shakespeare was transforming two other types of poem, the epithalamium and the *aubade*,
integrating them into moments where speakers were seeking to mark
life-altering events through poetic form. The epithalamium was a
poem spoken by a poet or the bridegroom to the bride on the evening
of their wedding. Shakespeare uses this form in Juliet's 'Gallop apace
you fiery footed steeds' (3.2.1). Gary McCown notes that 'Sir Philip
Sidney wrote the first epithalamium in English as a song which the
shepherd Dicus presents at the marriage of Thysis and Kala in the
third ecologue of *Arcadia*' (p. 152). It is a poem Shakespeare might
have known before he composed Juliet's speech. However, three stanzas from Edmund Spenser's 'Epithalamium' seem closer to what
Shakespeare wrote for Juliet. Spenser's poem was written for his marriage to Elizabeth Boyle, and these stanzas in the middle of the poem
mark the moment when day turns to night. The first stanza, with
its address to the maids accompanying the bride, provides an image
of the social ritual Juliet will not experience. The second, in which
the poet imagines himself alone with his bride, parallels the longing
expressed by Juliet. The third offers parallels with Juliet's invocation
of night. From *Edmund Spenser's Poetry* (2nd edition), edited by Hugh
Maclean (1982), pp. 500–1.

> Now ceasse ye damsels your delight forepast;
> Enough is it, that all the day is youres:
> Now day is doen, and night is nighing fast:
> Now bring the Bryde into the brydall boures.
> Now night is come, now soone her disarray,
> And in her bed her lay;
> Lay her in lillies and in violets,
> And silken courteins over her display,
> And odourd sheetes, and Arras coverlets.
> Behold how goodly my faire love does ly
> In proud humility;
> Like unto Maia, when as Jove her tooke,
> In Tempe, lying on the flowry gras,
> Twixt sleepe and wake, after she weary was,
> With bathing in Acidalian brooke.

Now it is night, ye damsels may be gon,
And leave my love alone,
And leave likewise your former lay to sing:
The woods no more shal answere, nor your echo ring.

Now welcome night, thou night so long expected,
That long daies labour doest at last defray,
And all my cares, which cruell love collected,
Hast sumd in one, and cancelléd for aye:
Spread thy broad wing over my love and me,
That no man may us see,
And in thy sable mantle us enwrap,
From feare of perrill and foule horror free.
Let no false treason seeke us to entrap,
Nor any dread disquiet once annoy
The safety of our joy:
But let the night be calme and quietsome,
Without tempestuous storms or sad affray:
Lyke as when Jove with fayre Alcmena lay,
When he begot the great Tirynthian groome:
Or like as when he with thy selfe did lie,
And begot Majesty.
And let the mayds and yongmen cease to sing:
Ne let the woods them answer, nor theyr eccho ring.

Let no lamenting cryes, nor dolefull teares,
Be heard all night within nor yet without:
Ne let false whispers, breeding hidden feares,
Breake gentle sleepe with misconceivéd dout.
Let no deluding dreames, nor dreadful sights
Make sudden sad affrights;
Ne let housefyres, nor lightnings helplesse harmes,
Ne let the Pouke, nor other evill sprights,
Ne let mischivous witches with theyr charmes,
Ne let hob Goblins, names whose sence we see not,
Fray us with things that be not.
Let not the shriech Oule, nor the Storke be heard:
Nor the night Raven that stil deadly yels,
Nor damnéd ghosts cald up with mighty spels,
Nor griesly vultures make us once affeard:
Ne let th'unpleasant Quyre of Frogs still croking
Make us wish theyr choking.
Let none of these theyr drery accents sing;
Ne let the woods them answer, nor theyr eccho ring.   (ll. 296–352)

Aubade

A third poetic form Shakespeare deployed was the *aubade* or dawn song, usually spoken by a man expressing regret that a night of love-making has gone by so quickly and day returned so soon. In the courtly love tradition in which the *aubade* originated, the speaker was obliged to leave in order to protect his married lover. Thus it is ironic that the newly-married Juliet and Romeo perform an *aubade*, but this irony registers the pressure created by their clandestine marriage. Shakespeare transforms this lyric by having it spoken by both Romeo and Juliet after their first and only night as husband and wife. John Donne's 'Break of Day' is interesting in relation to the dialogue of Romeo and Juliet since it seems to be spoken by a woman. The poem was written some time before 1612, was printed by William Corkine in his *Second Book of Airs*, and has been recorded by Paul Hillier (voice) and Nigel North (lute) on 'The Rags of Time' (Harmonia Mundi USA #907257). The text comes from *John Donne* edited by John Carey (1990), p. 102.

Break of Day

'Tis true, 'tis day, what though it be?
O wilt thou therefore rise from me?
Why should we rise, because 'tis light?
Did we lie down, because 'twas night?
Love which in spite of darkness brought us hither,
Should in despite of light keep us together.

Light hath no tongue, but is all eye;
If it could speak as well as spy,
This were the worst, that it could say,
That being well, I fain would stay,
And that I loved my heart and honour so,
That I would not from him, that had them, go.

Must business thee from hence remove?
Oh, that's the worst disease of love,
The poor, the foul, the false, love can
Admit, but not the busied man.
He which hath business, and makes love, doth do
Such wrong, as when a married man doth woo.

4   Key Productions

'Of all Shakespeare's plays', wrote William Hazlitt in his preface to Oxberry's 1819 edition of *Romeo and Juliet*, 'this is perhaps the one that is acted, if not the oftenest, with most pleasure to the spectator' (Levenson, 2000, p. 70). In London during the period from 1750 to 1800 it was performed 399 times, 'more than any other Shakespeare play' (Hogan, 1952, II, p. 716), and from 1970 to 2005 there were at least 40 productions in the United Kingdom (O'Connor and Goodland, 2007, pp. 1222–303). This chapter examines five productions. The first two, directed by David Garrick (1748 and 1750) and John Gielgud (1935), were the most influential versions of their respective eras. The third, *West Side Story* (1957 and 1961), had a powerful impact on the play's subsequent stage history. The last two are Michael Bogdanov's for the Royal Shakespeare Company (1986) and P.J. Papparelli's for the Folger Shakespeare Theatre (2005).

Romeo and Juliet, 1662–1747

Early in the Restoration, after Charles II licensed two theater companies and stipulated that women would perform the female roles, *Romeo and Juliet* was revived by Sir William Davenant on 1 March 1662, at Lincoln's-Inn-Fields, in a production that prompted Samuel Pepys to say it was 'a play of itself the worst that ever I heard in my life' (Levenson, 1987, p. 17). James Howard apparently composed a version with a happy ending, so that, as John Downes reports in *Roscius Anglicanus*, 'when the Tragedy was Reviv'd again 'twas Play'd Alternately, Tragical one Day, and Tragicomical another' (C3ᵛ, p. 22). In 1679 Thomas Otway introduced *The History and Fall of Caius Marius* using a plot based on Plutarch in which the lovers were the heirs of two Roman factions. Otway's enduring innovation was to have

Lavinia (Juliet) revive as Marius (Romeo) is dying, creating a short reunion before he expires and she stabs herself. Otway's version was performed 31 times by 1735 (*The London Stage*, IV, pp. 208–12). Theophilus Cibber produced a version at the Haymarket Theatre in September 1744, with himself, at age 40, as Romeo, and his daughter Jenny, at age 15, as Juliet. He used Shakespeare's text with elements from *Much Ado about Nothing* and Otway. His version had a short run before the authorities closed his unlicensed theater, and a letter from Garrick shows he considered this version 'tolerable enough' but thought the lovers poorly acted (Branam, 1984, p. 171).

David Garrick's production, 1748 and after

From 1748 until the middle of the nineteenth century, what spectators watched was some version of the adaptation produced by David Garrick in 1748 and revised in 1750. Garrick omitted the Choruses, cut about 850 lines, and added over 100, most in a scene between the temporarily reunited lovers (5.4.72–170). His version was designed to attract audiences whose sense of decorum presumed that tragic and comic, high and low, poetry and prose must be kept apart; that Romeo should love only Juliet; and that Juliet should not display the overt sexual desire that is a defining element of the role.

In his 1748 address 'To the Reader', Garrick explained that 'The Alterations in the following Play are few and trifling, except in the last Act; the Design was to clear the Original, as much as possible, from the Jingle and Quibble which were always thought the great Objection to reviving it' (Garrick, 1981, p. 77). Eliminating jingle meant eliminating rhyme, since blank verse was the proper medium for tragedy, and 'Garrick carefully removed as many of the approximately five hundred rhymes as he could rationalise' (Levenson, 1987, p. 22). Often he simply changed one rhyme word so that, for example, where the Friar remarks 'Jesu Maria, what a deal of brine/Hath washed thy sallow cheeks for Rosaline' (2.3.69–70), Garrick substitutes 'tears' for 'brine' (III.iii.51–2).

Eliminating 'quibble' meant eliminating puns. Samuel Johnson famously explained the supposedly deleterious effect of Shakespeare's word-play when he wrote that '[a] quibble, poor and barren as it is, gave him such delight, that he was content to purchase it, by the sacrifice of reason, propriety and truth' (VII, p. 74). In purifying the language, however, Garrick was also altering the characters. In the case of Mercutio, for example, he cut the sexually explicit lines in Queen Mab, the 'open-arse' speech, and speeches satirizing the Nurse, making possible the decorous fop created by Henry Woodward. But eliminating the puns also transformed Romeo since in omitting the wit-combat between Mercutio and Romeo he eliminated the scene which presents the Romeo for whose sake Mercutio is willing to die, undercutting first Mercutio's and then Romeo's motives for fighting Tybalt.

In transforming Juliet, Garrick eliminated almost all the overt sexuality. He made her 18, which was logical given that his first Juliet was the 34-year-old Susannah Cibber – but making her older underlined the fact that a woman was performing Juliet, which restored the sexuality excised from the language. The result of these maneuvers appears in the reduced sonnet:

> Romeo (*to Juliet*). If I profane with my unworthiest hand
>   This holy shrine, the gentle fine is this. (*Kiss.*)
> Juliet. Good pilgrim, you do wrong your hand too much,
>   For palm to palm is holy palmer's kiss.
> Romeo. Have not saints lips, and holy palmers too?
> Juliet. Ay, pilgrim, lips that they must use in prayer.
> Romeo. Thus then, dear saint, let lips put up their prayers. (*Kiss.*) (I.vi.61–7)

Ironically, this abbreviated dialogue prompted some critics to find Juliet too forward.

Even as he was simplifying the poetry Garrick was using the resources of his stage to enrich the spectacle. After his revival opened at Drury Lane on 29 November 1748, with Spranger Barry and Susanna Cibber as the lovers, the notice for the 1 December performance drew attention to the fact that it was appearing 'with a new *Masquerade Dance* proper to the Play'. In 1750 he replaced the mourning for Juliet with a funeral procession that included a dirge sung to music by William Boyce.

However, as happened in the volatile theatrical world of this period, Barry and Cibber moved to the rival house at Covent Garden, where John Rich planned to open the 1750–51 season with Garrick's stars in Garrick's version. Garrick secretly began to rehearse with 18-year-old George Ann Bellamy playing Juliet while he learned

Romeo. The competition began on 28 September 1750 and continued for 11 further performances through 20 October, after which the
Covent Garden production ceased and Garrick offered one more performance. The most often-cited distinction between the Romeos is a
comment attributed to the actress Hannah Pritchard, who said 'Had
I been Juliet to Garrick's Romeo, – so ardent and impassioned was he,
I should have expected he would have *come up* to me in the balcony;
but had I been Juliet to Barry's Romeo, – so tender, so eloquent, and so
seductive was he, I should certainly have *gone down* to him!' (Burnim,
1973, pp. 131–2). The consensus was that Garrick was finer as the tragic
hero and Barry was supreme as the lover. Cibber was judged to be
supreme in projecting Juliet's suffering and Bellamy projected more
amorous energy.

In his 1753 Advertisement Garrick explained his 75-line addition in
the final scene as follows:

> Bandello, the Italian novelist from whom Shakespeare has borrowed the
> subject of this play, has made Juliet to wake in the tomb before Romeo
> dies: this circumstance Shakespeare has omitted, not perhaps from judg-
> ment, but from reading the story in the French or English translation, both
> which had injudiciously left out this addition to the catastrophe.
>
> (Garrick, 1981, p. 79)

Garrick wrote the scene so that the actor playing Romeo could produce a display of the passions. The record also indicates differences
in how each Juliet performed this scene: Cibber was criticized for
waking 'instantaneously', diminishing the acting opportunities for
Romeo, while Bellamy won praise for careful gradations of returning
consciousness which enabled Garrick to develop Romeo's changes.
But when she stabbed herself Cibber 'introduced a shudder that
affects the whole audience' (Burnim, p. 209).

Finally, as Loehlin notes (2002, p. 14), Garrick's dialogue emphasized the feud as the dying Romeo proclaimed 'Fathers have flinty
hearts, no tears can melt 'em./Nature pleads in vain – children must
be wretched' (p. 144), and was echoed by the Prince:

> Well may you mourn, my lords, now wise too late,
> These tragic issues of your mutual hate.
> From private feuds, what dire misfortunes flow;
> Whate'er the cause, the sure effect is woe.   (V.iv.250–3, p. 148)

In Garrick's version, and, in particular, in Barry's performance, Romeo became what his name still denotes, the epitome of the romantic lover (Wright, 1997, pp. 88–90).

John Gielgud's 1935 production

John Gielgud brought to his production highly developed skills as an actor and emerging skills as a director. He had achieved fame by both acting in and directing a notable production of *Hamlet* which had run for 155 performances (Gielgud, 1991, p. 9). He was one of the first director's to grasp that 'The whole beauty of the plays lies in their construction', and that '[a]fter 300 years we're just discovering how they ought to be played' (Levenson, 1987, p. 47). That construction needed to be rediscovered because in the nineteenth century a drive for historically accurate settings combined with new technologies had produced stagings so elaborate that 'scene-changing could swallow as much as three-quarters of an hour in a night' (Trewin, 1964, p. 4). This problem was often solved by playing the scenes on a set one after the other, so that a production of *The Merchant of Venice* might perform 'all the early Venice scenes . . . followed by the early Belmont scenes' (Trewin, p. 18). This solution, however, destroyed the pattern by which alternate locations create meaning by juxtaposing multiple plots. In his experiments, William Poel began to recover this pattern, and this recovery gained momentum in Harley Granville-Barker's productions and *Prefaces*. Gielgud's set was designed by the team of three women – Margaret and Sophia Harris, and Elizabeth Montgomery – known as 'Motley', who created a central tower flanked by two arches with open areas for acting, a rostrum for the bedroom, and a cell wheeled on as needed (Levenson, 1987, pp. 57–60). A.V. Cookman (*The New York Times*, 17 November 1935), wrote that 'the production itself achieved a rare measure of speed and balance, continuously keeping vivid the contrast between scene and scene which is Shakespeare's most obvious technical device in this tragedy and at the same time preserving the close connection between the lovers' course and the progress of their parents' feud'.

Gielgud managed another innovation by persuading Laurence Olivier to join him rather than mount his own production: they opened with Olivier as Romeo and Gielgud as Mercutio and switched

after six weeks. Gielgud insisted that proper verse-speaking was
essential (*The Evening Standard*, 10 October 1935, quoted by Levenson,
1987, p. 51):

> I want to see Romeo and Juliet in contrast to the other characters – poetry
> in contrast to prose. I want to set them almost on an operatic plane so that
> they shall *sing* those marvelous duets while the other characters *speak* their
> lines. . . . They must not only be Romeo and Juliet: they must be symbolic,
> immortal types of the lovers of all time.

Olivier worked from a different premise:

> I've always thought that [Gielgud and I] were the reverses of the same coin,
> perhaps. I've seen, as if you had a coin, the top half John . . . all spirituality,
> all beauty, all abstract things; and myself as all earth, blood, human-
> ity . . . I've always felt that John missed the lower half and that made me go
> for the other . . . when I was playing Romeo . . . I was trying to sell realism
> in Shakespeare.   (Burton, 1967, p. 17)

Some reviews were so severe that Olivier offered to resign the role,
but his offer was not accepted, and other observers praised his innovations. '[H]e won half his battle as soon as Romeo, the olive-skinned,
impetuous adolescent, entered straight from Renaissance Italy, a
world of hot sun, sharp swords, and brief lives' (Trewin, 1964, p. 153).
He 'was ridiculed for his adolescent postures and leaps below Juliet's
balcony' (Wright, p. 214) but what appalled some enthralled others:
'[h]is beautiful pose as he stood beneath the balcony expressed the
essence of the character to perfection' (Gielgud, p. 48). Some reviewers criticized his speaking, but others heard telling modulations: 'he
caressed certain phrases ("Look, love, what envious streaks Do lace
the severing clouds in yonder east") as no other player had done'
(Trewin, p. 153). In the tomb he added the new business of 'having Romeo dying stretch out his hand toward Juliet, whose hand, as
she stirred in her sleep, almost touched, but did not quite touch his'
(Sprague, 1963, p. 319). 'Romeo played as neither a brooding tragic
figure nor a gallant, but rather as a boy exuberantly in love' was
Olivier's creation (Wright, p. 195). Gielgud's Romeo elicited contrasting praise. Charles Morgan wrote that 'The exaltation itself is . . . not
hot, not animal, but lyrically passionate, having precisely the same
relationship to physical desire as song has to a prose piece with the

same subject' (*The New York Times*, 29 November 1935). Wright suggests audiences witnessed what 'was probably the last time a great actor spoke the lines in the grand, romantic tradition begun by Spranger Barry almost two hundred years before' (p. 217).

There was also a contrast between their Mercutios. Gielgud wrote 'I knew I was more lyrically successful as Mercutio in the Queen Mab scene, but his virility and panache in the other scenes, his furious and skillful fencing and final exit to his death, were certainly more striking in the part than anything I was able to achieve' (p. 48). Olivier's Mercutio 'got a great deal of fun from taunting Juliet's nurse and on the line, "A sail, a sail..!" he scandalized her by lifting her billowing skirts on the point of his sword' (Barker, 1953, p. 71).

Edith Evans played the Nurse swathed in a costume which focused attention on her expressive face and her remarkable voice. 'Coarse, garrulous, wordy, dominant, massive with the accretions of an experience that has left her fundamentally shallow-pated, it is a mighty achievement in characterization never irritatingly elaborated, and in elocution governed continually by internal word-sense' (Farjeon, 1949, p. 122).

Peggy Ashcroft was a youthful-looking 28, and critics described her as being childlike in all but her love for Romeo:

> It is a frightened child who is shaken with fears of what hideous spectres may meet her eyes when she wakens in the tomb: a woman strong on the wings of passion who, mastering childish fears, cries 'Romeo, I come! this do I drink to thee.' So it is almost continuously, the child and the woman integral parts of the same character, a performance of rare fitness to the play.   (Cookman)

Judi Dench's performance in Zeffirelli's 1960 revival prompted W.A. Darlington to recall Ashcroft's Juliet (*The Daily Telegraph*, 17 October 1960, quoted by Levenson, 1987, p. 53):

> When Dame Peggy played it in 1935 the audience ... was not at all silent. There was an almost continuous murmur, built up by the small sounds of appreciation made by the individuals as the actress, by minute inflections of her voice, conjured up unexpected felicities from the familiar words.

> For instance, on the words 'I have forgot why I did call thee back', Dame Peggy was rewarded by a burst of sympathetic and spontaneous laughter.

> There was in her voice a happy realisation that any reason Juliet may have
> given herself for recalling Romeo had been no more than an excuse.

Gielgud's production ran for 189 performances setting a new record
for this play (Trewin, p. 152), and contributed to the recovery of something approaching the original staging. The contrast between Gielgud
and Olivier in both roles contributed to a shift in how actors spoke the
verse, and Olivier's Romeo and Mercutio set the stage for the more
sexual and violent realizations in subsequent productions. Edith
Evans was still performing her Nurse in 1961 and Ashcroft's success
spotlighted the challenge for actresses to make Juliet a convincing
adolescent yet project the complexity of her speeches.

West Side Story, 1957 and 1961

West Side Story opened at the Winter Garden Theater in New York City
on 26 September 1957. This adaptation was developed from a con-
cept by Jerome Robbins, with a book by Arthur Laurents, music by
Leonard Bernstein, and lyrics by Stephen Sondheim. A film directed
by Robbins and Robert Wise was released in 1961:

> *West Side Story*'s enduring reputation has come about, by general agree-
> ment, because of the film ... which won numerous Academy Awards,
> including Best Picture. The score became popular largely because of the
> film's expensive advertising campaign. Music the critics had pronounced
> interesting but not 'hummable' turned out to be unforgettable because,
> Sondheim pointed out, people had had a chance to get to like it.
>
> (Secrest, 1998, p. 126)

West Side Story was a pivotal event in the history of Shakespeare's play,
such that '[i]n the later half of the twentieth century *Romeo and Juliet*
was transformed, in production and perception, from a play about
love into a play about hate' (Loehlin, 2002, p. 66).

It is hard to recapture the impact of *West Side Story* in part because
gang warfare has become so much more lethal and the representation
of such conflict has become so much more graphic that its violence
looks tame. Our evolving understanding of the causes, malignancy,
and persistence of gangs, moreover, means that its message – that tol-
erance can dissolve bigotry and hatred (Laurents, 2009, pp. 146, 158,

169–70) – has come to seem oversimplified. However, the show's contemporary impact is registered in Brooks Atkinson's review, where he
wrote that 'the material is horrifying', that 'very little of the hideous-
ness has been left out', and that the team had composed 'a profoundly
moving show that is as ugly as the city jungles and also pathetic,
tender and forgiving' (Beckerman, 1973, p. 385). In transforming the
feuding houses of Verona into the teenage gangs of mid-twentieth-
century New York City, Laurents supplied a content that Shakespeare
did not:

> The cause of the West Side Manhattan gangs' rivalry is completely clear:
> it is between first generation Americans whose security ... they feel to
> be jeopardized by the Puerto Ricans ... and the newcomers, fighting to
> establish themselves in an alien community. The tooth-and-nail defense
> of the former's tenuous priority is bound to force a tooth-and-nail
> reaction.   (Houghton, 1965, p. 12)

This reframing prompted other changes, some hinted at in the cast
list that named 'The Jets' and 'Their Girls', 'The Sharks' and 'Their
Girls', and 'The Adults'. First, the gangs are united primarily by eth-
nicity and language rather than family. Second, while Tony and Maria
refer to their parents, those parents never appear, and the only adults
are Detective Schrank and Officer Krupke, despised by both gangs;
Glad Hand, the social worker whose effort to bring the gangs together
provides the opportunity for Tony and Maria to fall in love; and Doc,
who owns the drugstore where the Jets meet and where Tony hides
after killing Bernardo. Third, each gang had a set of 'girls', and the
presence of the Shark girls meant that, unlike Juliet, Maria is part of a
group of young women with whom she can share her life even as she
tries to hide her secret. Fourth, Laurents made Bernardo, the leader of
the Sharks, Maria's older brother, not her cousin, and gave Bernardo a
girlfriend, Anita, who is Maria's best friend and a crucial figure in the
plot. For where the Nurse saves the lovers from being discovered by
Lady Capulet, Anita discovers that Maria has just made love with Tony
and she faces her own tragic dilemma when Maria asks her to warn
Tony that she will be delayed in joining him for their escape. Anita
goes to Doc's store, but when she is taunted and sexually assaulted
by the Jets, she seeks revenge by saying that Chino, Maria's fiancé, has
killed Maria – a lie that impels Tony to roam the streets pleading for
Chino to kill him.

Setting the story in mid-twentieth-century New York City meant replacing Shakespeare's poetry and prose with the vernacular of hip teenagers and square adults. What was lost in linguistic power was replaced, in part, by the dances choreographed by Robbins in response to Bernstein's propulsive score, and these dances filled the stage and the screen with an energy like the 'whiz-bang exhilarating kinesthesia of speed and clash' essential to *Romeo and Juliet* (Goldman, 1972, p. 33). Indeed Atkinson praised the way

> Everything contributes to the total impression of wildness, ecstasy, and anguish. . . . the ballets convey the things that Mr. Laurents is inhibited from saying because the characters are so inarticulate. The hostility and suspicion between the gangs, the glory of the nuptials, the terror of the rumble, the devastating climax – Mr. Robbins has found the patterns of movement that express these parts of the story.   (Beckerman, p. 386)

If it is in the dances that hate is most forcefully expressed, the love is most movingly articulated in 'some of the most gorgeous love songs ever' written, including 'Maria', 'Tonight', and 'the musical's banner anthem, the aching "Somewhere" ' (Ben Brantley, *The New York Times*, 20 March 2009). In *West Side Story*, 'Somewhere' serves as the anthem which expresses a faith that the world can be transformed by love. In concerts and recordings, moreover, it has become an anthem which – like Judy Garland's 'Somewhere over the Rainbow' from *The Wizard of Oz* – expresses the fantasy that a better world would materialize if the lovers could simply join hands and move toward the horizon.

Yet as Laurents points out 'for a show that relies so much on song and dance, there is neither in the last half of the second act' (2009, p. 146), and it is through dialogue that he modifies Shakespeare's climax, starting with making Anita's vengeful lie rather than Balthazar's innocent mistake the act that triggers the ending. Here the mistiming occurs when Tony sees Maria just seconds before Chino shoots him. As in Garrick's version, Romeo and Juliet are reunited, but there is only time for a brief reprise of 'Somewhere' as Tony dies in Maria's arms. In Shakespeare, Romeo's death prompts Juliet to commit suicide, but Tony's death prompts Maria to seize the gun from Chino and turn it on the gang members as she cries 'I can kill now because *I* hate now.' As she points the gun at Action (a Jet) while asking 'How many can I kill, Chino? How many – and still have one bullet left for me?' (p. 224), she conjures a startling image of Juliet committing homicide before suicide, producing a pile of corpses surpassing the carnage at the end of *Romeo and Juliet*. Instead, she drops the gun to move into an ending at once more and less hopeful than Shakespeare's. It seems more hopeful because she chooses to live; because one of the Jets 'comes forward to pick up Maria's shawl and put it over her head' (p. 224); and because members of both gangs carry off Tony's body. It seems less hopeful insofar as the final stage direction mandates that '*The adults . . . are left bowed, alone, useless*' (p. 224). Not only are the adults helpless to prevent tragedy and useless to resolve the conditions that generate it, but they are indicted as the cause of the problem:

Doc: What does it take to get through to you? When do you stop?
    You make this world lousy!
Action: That's the way we found it, Doc. (II.iv, p. 219)

In the movie, Action replies 'We didn't make it, Doc', and in both versions his words echo the moment when Garrick's Romeo indicts the older generation, even as his sweeping judgment foreshadows developments in later productions of *Romeo and Juliet*.

West Side Story initiated a shift in which '[m]odern productions [of *Romeo and Juliet*] tended to emphasize the feud over the love story, and have used it to comment on a variety of social ills: from the competitiveness and greed of the parents, to the sexual aggression of young men, to ethnic or cultural difference as a source of conflict' (Loehlin, 2002, p. 66). This maneuver has also served to rectify the alleged weakness many critics think makes *Romeo and Juliet* a failed tragedy (see Critical Assessments): when the ancient grudge is recreated as an intractable conflict, it is not the stars but the social order itself that produces the outcome. However, while reshaping the play so that it embodies an intractable conflict creates a powerful sense of tragic inevitability, it risks reducing the lovers to victims – a tension that haunts some subsequent productions.

Michael Bogdanov's 1986 RSC production

Michael Bogdanov's production opened at the Royal Shakespeare Theatre on 10 April 1986 and built on *West Side Story* and Zeffirelli, setting the play in 1986 Italy, where 'Capulet . . . became a self-made tycoon and the Prince a sinister trench-coated figure in dark glasses

accompanied by minders' (Jackson, 2002, p. 42). It produced enthu-
siastic audiences and diverse reviews. Nicholas Shrimpton wrote
that '[t]he text was cut to ribbons ... [and w]hat remained was
buried beneath a torrent of modernity [in which] Verona was the
fashionable glossy magazine Italy ... and the ... two hours traffic of
the stage became ... a procession of real motor-bikes and sports
cars' (1987, p. 178). For Gerald Berkowitz, 'Bogdanov's modern dress
Romeo and Juliet was the sort of updating that enrages purists and
thrills audiences, making the play come alive without patronizing it'
(1987, p. 497).

Bogdanov is a director committed to exposing the workings of
power which he believes modern audiences miss because they are
distracted by Shakespeare's status as a classic and by the beauty of
language. His 1978 *Taming of the Shrew*, for example, began with an
iconoclastic act in which a drunken man (who became Petruchio)
climbed onto the stage and began tearing down the set, while an
usher (who became Katherina) failed to stop him. Thus Bogdanov and
designer Chris Dyer created an experience in which '[t]he scenogra-
phy ... was a visualization of Brecht's "Not ... but" process: not then
but now, not illusion but truth, not painted perspective but hard
iron railings, not Serlio but Dyer. And, a traditionalist might add, not
Shakespeare but Bogdanov' (Kennedy, 1993, p. 3). In *Romeo* Bogdanov
used his opening to challenge the audience but saved his more radical
re-scripting for the end:

> As we enter the Stratford theatre, a rock group is playing mood-indigo
> music, a black guy is cruising round the marble-smooth stage on roller-
> skates, and there is a pervasive whiff of black leather. ... And [later] as
> Benvolio arrives on a motor-bike and Tybalt turns up in the Veronese
> Square in a low-slung red sports car, it becomes impossible not to dub
> this the Alfa Romeo and Juliet.   (Billington, 1993, p. 254)

Their opulence, however, could not hide the tensions in the Capulet
family. At their 'ghastly poolside party' (Warren, p. 85), Anna Nygh's
Lady Capulet danced with Hugh Quarshie's Tybalt, with whom she
was having an affair. Tybalt addressed 'This by his voice should be
a Montague' to her, and his 'Patience' speech to Capulet, and exited,
with Lady Capulet following him after casting a 'withering look at
her husband' (Jackson, p. 55). In 3.1, 'Capulet slapped his wife's face
after she had knelt to make her impassioned plea to the Prince;'

in 3.4, when he tried to embrace her as he told Paris they loved Tybalt 'she turned away from him;' and when he tried to embrace her after arranging the marriage with Paris '[s]he walked off on the opposite side of the stage' (Jackson, p. 56). Finally, in 4.2, after Juliet agreed to marry Paris, Lady Capulet approached Capulet with papers, but he said 'I'll not to bed tonight, let me alone', and in response she 'crumpled her papers, threw them at him, and walked off' (Jackson, p. 59). These scenes demonstrated why Juliet, as Niamh Cusack explains, 'looks at her mother and thinks "I won't be like that"' (Cusack, 1988, p. 125). What she witnesses prompted her to reject Paris, and to find Romeo appealing because their rapport promises a loving union that would also liberate her from parental control.

Michael Kitchen 'was an aging and melancholy Mercutio, no longer able to believe in the childish games of this group but unable to escape them, taking refuge in drink, affectionate patronizing of Romeo' (Berkowitz, 1987, p. 497). He performed the Queen Mab speech as a bedtime story, with Romeo seated on his knee, sucking his thumb like an infant. With the Nurse in 2.2 his impulse to humiliate others came to the fore:

> Kitchen ... who has been kissing the hand of Dilys Laye's faux-genteel Nurse, placed it on his crotch, and she withdrew it angrily. He used his cane to flick washing off the basket on the back of her tricycle, then poked her with it as she tried to gather the scattered garments, pushing her down onto all fours and sitting astride her. As he left he kissed her on 'Farewell' then added 'ancient lady'.
> (Jackson, 2002, p. 108)

In the fight 'Kitchen spelt out his insults to Tybalt with an unmistakably contemptuous emphasis on the initial consonants ... and responded to Tybalt's "I am for you sir" ... by kicking him in the crotch.' The turning point came when Mercutio and Tybalt 'toasted each other, but Tybalt threw the contents of his glass in his adversary's face' (Jackson, 2002, p. 114).

Critics disagreed about Niamh Cusack and Sean Bean. Billington thought that 'Cusacks's Juliet has possibilities ... but her voice lacks texture and colour: the same goes for Sean Bean's likeable but raw Romeo' (1993, p. 256). Roger Warren suggested that

> The great virtue of Sean Bean's Romeo was that he was completely unafraid of his conceited language. ... His elaborate oxymorons ...

emerged as Romeo's attempt to express confused feelings. He became increasingly convincing and sympathetic, especially in the balcony scene with Niamh Cusack's attractively honest, direct Juliet.   (1987, p. 85)

Gerald Berkowitz, who saw the play in Stratford and reviewed it after it transferred to the Barbican in London (14 April 1987), was not impressed:

> Unfortunately, the two key roles were a disappointment, leaving some-thing of a vacuum at the center of the play. Sean Bean's Romeo had deepened a bit since Stratford, where I thought him never more than a self-pitying wimp; at least he was able to suggest a few moments of delight in the balcony scene as unexpected eloquence came to his aid. But Niamh Cusack's Juliet, who had seemed in Stratford to develop nicely from touch-ing innocence to unexpected reserves of strength, was now all one-note, both figuratively and literally; her voice had a very narrow range that made everything sound the same, shallow and dispassionate.   (p. 498)

Whatever Bogdanov's intent, it can be argued that 'a vacuum at the center of the play' served his purpose insofar as it underlined the fact that '[t]he lovers were wholly [society's] victims' and that '[i]t was less their tragedy than that of a violent, brutal world in whose materialistic values lay the seeds of its own destruction' (Warren, 1987, p. 85).

Bogdanov's most radical re-scripting created a striking ending:

> After Juliet's death, the stage was darkened; when the lights came up, the audience saw the Prince reading most of the opening choric sonnet (switched to the past tense) from note cards while standing in front of two golden statues. When this Mafia don finished, photographers ran down the theatre aisles, snapping pictures first of him, then of Montague and Capulet shaking hands, then of various combinations involving the wives (so Lady Montague is not dead), the friar, the nurse, even the apothecary, so that what we saw was a press conference and photo session after an unveiling. After some perfunctory mourning and laying of flowers, the final image was that of Benvolio going off alone, disconsolate (the only show of real emotion).   (Dessen, 1987, p. 95)

By omitting the Chorus before the first scene and having the Prince deliver its first eight lines as a press release, Bogdanov insured that this frame was discredited by the self-interested motives of the speaker

and corrupt acts of the survivors. For Bogdanov, '[e]recting gold statues won't change anything' (2003, p. 33) and the idea that the lovers
were doomed by society's values was precisely the conclusion he
wanted the spectators to reach.

P.J. Paparelli's 2005 Folger Theatre production

P.J. Papparelli's *Romeo and Juliet* opened at the Folger Theatre at the
Folger Shakespeare Library in Washington, D.C., on 12 January 2005.
Papparelli situated his production in Shakespeare's Verona but also,
as his program explained, in the context of events such as the 1999
Columbine massacre, in which two teenage boys at Columbine High
School in Littleton, Colorado killed 12 students and one teacher, and
wounded 23 more people before shooting themselves. Interviewing
teenagers around the United States, Paparelli saw a world in which
children seemed left to raise themselves and had trouble connecting
with surrogates who might help them become stable adults.

The play began with a version of the prologue which became
the cue for an extra-textual epilogue. Three women entered and
began washing the bloodstained floor, and were gradually joined by
the rest of the cast, with people speaking a line or part of a line
until the ensemble performed the couplet, memorializing their city's
history of violence. That violence – vividly choreographed by Paul
Dennhardt – was linked by a powerful visual motif. The servants of
the opening scene were pre-adolescent children and Sampson, the
smallest of the four, was severely beaten by the two Montague servants, while those who came to his aid tried to compress and bandage
his wounds. In 3.1 Romeo and Benvolio tried to compress Mercutio's
wound, just as the Capulets tried to compress Tybalt's.

The Capulets were a wealthy family favored by the Prince who,
in several extra-textual appearances, encouraged the match between
Paris and Juliet, and thus helped motivate Capulet's harsh attack on
Juliet when she refused to comply. Montague was a single parent,
and when he said 'Black and portentous must this humor prove' his
words resonated in a society facing high levels of teenage homicide
and suicide.

Graham Hamilton's Romeo was less a Petrarchan lover than 'a sen-
sitive youth, but a callow hurried one' (Trey Graham, *Washington's*

City Paper, 21 January 2005), and that haste was apparent when he cut himself on the dagger the Friar used to gather plants. Nicole Lowrence's Juliet was an adolescent 'who swings from girlish rapture to surprising resolve to coltish panic as events get more complicated' (Graham). She began her first scene engaged in a pillow fight with a servant but at her mother's approach arranged herself in bed in a demure pose and remained outwardly obedient. When she and the Nurse were alone, they laughed, hugged, and celebrated her sexuality by spreading their legs while giggling with delight. Juliet later performed this gesture to convince the Nurse she was happy to marry Paris, and the Nurse repeated it as she tried to wake Juliet for the wedding. In the potion scene Juliet took the drug early, asked 'What if it be a poison?' (4.3.23), and tried but failed to vomit. When the drug suddenly took effect, her harshly labored breathing recalled how teenagers die from drugs overdoses.

In his review, Graham wrote of the Friar and Nurse that 'These are people deeply attached to and deeply fearful for, their headstrong charges, people who try hard and try repeatedly to steer the central twosome through a situation that needn't be as impossible as it seems', and the most vivid instance of their effort took place in the Friar's cell. The scene began with the agitated Romeo on stage as the Friar entered with a lantern, which he placed on the ground. Explaining to Romeo that he had received '[a] gentler judgement' (l. 10), a tender smile played on his lips as he touched Romeo's shoulder, but that touch prompted Romeo to express his fury (l. 19) with a blow which propelled the lantern upstage. The Friar opened the grate where he stored his plants and dagger and picked up a bible, but another blow sent the book spinning upstage (l. 58). In despair (l. 70) Romeo curled into a ball as the Friar tried to make him hide. When the Friar let the Nurse in, he showed, by gesture and speech, that it was her turn to deal with this problem child. Her commands (ll. 90–1) got Romeo to his feet but as he spoke (ll. 101–7) he raced to the grate, grabbed the dagger, and slashed his wrist.

Both adults were appalled, and the Friar cried out (l. 107), rushed downstage, and, as he compressed and bandaged the wound, asked 'Art thou a man?' (l. 108). While the fact that Romeo had killed Tybalt had not shaken the Friar's faith, now he had to confront Romeo's willingness to commit suicide and abandon Juliet. At line 135 he cradled Romeo's head in his hands, and when he came to line 144 the heavily stressed iteration expressed a fear that nothing he could say or do might save Romeo. While the Nurse gave Romeo the ring which completed his revival (ll. 160–4), the Friar walked downstage, grasped the cross he wore, and revised his strategy. When Romeo moved toward the Friar he wanted an embrace to reassure him there had been no change in their relationship. Three times (ll. 165–70), however, the Friar prevented that embrace, finally compelling a handshake (l. 171) intended to insure Romeo did not regress again. Romeo reluctantly moved upstage, picked up the bible, and hugged it to his chest: it was now a symbol of the consolation he had earlier rejected and a substitute for the embrace he had not received.

One consequence of this staging was that the partial rupture between Romeo and the Friar paralleled the absolute rupture between Juliet and the Nurse. The choices here also inflected later scenes. Given Romeo's slashed wrist, the Friar's dismay when Juliet drew her dagger had particular urgency, and when he offered her the potion he was using it to secure the dagger. When the Friar rebuked Juliet's parents (4.4.91–109) his face revealed how guilt-ridden he was, and this was confirmed when Friar John found Laurence pounding his breast while silently saying 'Mea Culpa, mea culpa, mea maxima culpa!' His guilt was underlined when he witnessed Romeo's final agony and abandoned Juliet, and his final plea expressed a genuine desire to be held accountable for his mistakes (5.3.266–9).

In the tomb, the leitmotif of violence was completed. After she watched Romeo die and the Friar flee, Juliet found a dagger, stabbed herself and then cut her throat. She was still alive as her horrified parents tried to compress her wounds during her dying spasms. Finally, the four servants from the opening fight found the dagger and, kneeling, held it up before the lights went out. We could not tell if they were thinking 'Violence! Cool!' or 'Not a good idea!' but the bloodstains were in place to prompt the washing ritual that opened the performance, suggesting an endless cycle of violence.

The production elicited diametrically opposed reviews. For Nicholas F. Benton, the pivotal scene was Capulet's savage attack on Juliet for refusing to marry Paris, and the production was a moving exploration of 'an all too familiar kind of parental abuse' (*Falls Church News-Press*, 20 January 2005, p. 27). In *The Washington Times* (21 January 2005), however, T.L Ponick scornfully described the younger generation as 'a batch of rich, immature, violence-prone, hyper-emotional teen-agers, with a little too much time on their hands and more hor-mones than brains'. Ponick also claimed that 'depending on your age', Mercutio, for example, 'is either your best high school friend in 2005, or a total pain in the tush if you're a parent' (D8), but he also showed how responses could be shaped by gender as well as generation when his scorn for the young men was balanced by his admiration for 'Nicole Lowrence's star turn as a sweetly "tweeny" but ultimately tragic Juliet' (D8). In his indictment of society Papparelli echoed *West Side Story*, but in the Friar and the Nurse he presented adults who were not 'useless' but rather trying to supply the guidance not supplied by the parents of Juliet and Romeo.

5   The Play on Screen

Film versions of *Romeo and Juliet* differ from stage versions because the medium is not the actor's voice and body but film itself. In a film some of Shakespeare's language will be replaced by physical action, and that action will be shaped by the camera's capacity to control what we see. When watching a theatrical performance we are free to look at anything happening anywhere on stage: at the climax of *Hamlet*, most of us will focus on the duel between Hamlet and Laertes, so that when Shakespeare wants us to attend to the dying Queen he has Osric cry 'Look to the Queen there ho' (V.ii.303) – before Horatio directs attention to Hamlet, Osric directs attention to Laertes, and her own speech directs attention to Gertrude's final words to Hamlet. In addition, the filmmaker can use the camera so that we have no choice but to look at the Queen and no option to look at anyone else, no matter how urgently we wish to see their reaction. There is, moreover, a tension between the two mediums insofar as Shakespeare wrote for a stage where words create the setting while film excels at showing fully realized locations. So the film director must decide whether to keep the Friar's description of gathering plants or simply show him doing so, and whether to keep the comment on 'grace and rude will' (2.2.28) which can frame Romeo. Filmmakers can also invent ways to realize Shakespeare's images, as when the play's 'fourteen references to the sun' become embodied when Zeffirelli's prologue shows the sun over Verona (Rothwell, 1999, p. 135).

Film versions of *Romeo and Juliet* include those directed by George Cukor (1936), Renato Castellani (1954), Franco Zeffirelli (1968), and Baz Luhrmann (1996), and there is Alvin Rakoff's television production in the BBC-Time/Life series (1978). This chapter focuses on the films by Cukor, Zeffirelli, and Luhrmann.

George Cukor, 1936

In 1935 Irving Thalberg of Metro-Goldwyn-Mayer secured the then lavish sum of $2 million to produce *Romeo and Juliet* in a version starring his wife, Norma Shearer, and the English actor Leslie Howard. Thalberg selected George Cukor to direct, Talbot Jennings to write the screenplay, and William Strunk of Cornell University to be a literary advisor – and this version preserves more of the text than do the Zeffirelli and Luhrmann films. Using research brought back from Verona, the studio constructed a spacious version of the central square for the outdoor scenes, as well as a massive ballroom and a spectacular garden for the Capulet mansion. Costumes were based on Renaissance art, much of the music was from the period, and Agnes de Mille choreographed a dance sequence for Juliet. In short, Thalberg and Cukor sought to produce a cinematic equivalent of the pictorial productions that dominated the late-nineteenth-century stage. This was a paradigm that introduced live rabbits in *A Midsummer Night's Dream*, and one sign of Cukor's fidelity to this paradigm comes when the camera finds Juliet in the garden 'feeding a pet deer' (Buhler, 2002, p. 62).

The budget also enabled Thalberg and Cukor to hire a cast of American and British stars which, in addition to Shearer and Howard, included John Barrymore as Mercutio, Basil Rathbone as Tybalt, Edna May Oliver as the Nurse, C. Aubrey Smith as Capulet, Violet Kemball Cooper as Lady Capulet, and Andy Devine as Peter. The casting followed nineteenth-century theatrical conventions in employing older actors to play the younger generation because of their verse-speaking skill. Even in 1936, however, having mature actors perform the lovers on stage was becoming problematic, and the harsher lighting and the intimacy of the camera made it impossible to ignore the fact that Howard, at 42, and Shearer, at 35, were mature adults who neither looked like adolescents nor moved with an adolescent's gravity-defying energy. Especially in early scenes 'when she tries to skip and simper her way into Juliet's youth', Shearer almost seems childish rather than girlish, giving no hint of her later decisive behavior (Buhler, p. 62).

Working within this paradigm Cukor did, however, produce some vivid scenes. For example, where the Chorus tells us that we will see 'two households, both alike in dignity', Cukor staged the opening riot

as triggered not by the encounter of four servants but as a consequence of having processions of Montagues and Capulets converge as
they approach the cathedral. The result is a scene in which a sequence
of 'forty or so shots from a variety of camera angles' demonstrates the
feud's potential for unleashing public disorder (Rothwell, p. 42). The
Capulet feast shows how film could amplify nineteenth-century stage
practice in creating spectacle. The feast takes place in a huge ball-
room, and the extensive dance sequence choreographed by Agnes de
Mille can seem more appropriate to a musical than to a Shakespeare
play, presenting Juliet almost as if she were a prima ballerina. This
scene also demonstrates that the movie 'is from first to last a show-
case for its Juliet', and from this scene onward the camera often gazes
at Juliet in a way that merges our gaze with the adoring gaze of Romeo
(Buhler, p. 61). This rapt gaze tends to objectify Juliet and to down-
play the fact that much of the time it is her choices which drive the
action. Looking back, it seems ironic that Cukor was directing this
film even as John Gielgud was directing a production that dropped
the nineteenth-century paradigm in order to approach the spare, fluid
staging at the core of Shakespeare's dramaturgy. Looking forward,
we can see that in its lavish settings, opening riot, extended dance,
and luxurious garden, Cukor's film anticipates key elements in the
Zeffirelli and Luhrmann films. What this film could not anticipate
was how the transformation in the idea of adolescence as a separate life-phase and the emergence of the baby-boom generation of
teenagers would impel Zeffirelli to cast much younger actors to play
the lovers.

Franco Zeffirelli, 1960 and 1968

When Franco Zeffirelli came to direct his film of *Romeo and Juliet*,
he had already directed an influential production of the play for
the Old Vic Theatre (1960) and directed a film of *The Taming of the
Shrew* (1966) starring Elizabeth Taylor and Richard Burton. That film
grossed over $2 million and his *Romeo* became 'the most popular
and financially successful Shakespeare film yet made' (Jorgens, 1977,
p. 80). In directing his first Shakespeare play, Zeffirelli aimed to produce 'a combination of Italian feeling applied to a masterpiece of the
classical English theater' (Zeffirelli, 1976, pp. 437–8). He thought of

Shakespeare as 'a frustrated traveler', and saw himself as taking the audience on the 'trip to Italy' Shakespeare could only have imagined and his stage could never have presented (p. 439). He also acknowledged that '[d]irection is not pure creation' because '[y]ou take somebody else's conception and you have to respect it', and added '[y]ou don't need many ideas, you need one' (p. 439). He seized the idea in *West Side Story* and his Verona was plagued by a gang-like feud made worse by the older generation's futile efforts to control a younger generation they were incapable of understanding or nurturing.

Levenson records that 'the Old Vic asked Zeffirelli to stage *Romeo and Juliet* for two reasons: his recent success directing opera at Covent Garden, as well as the theatre's interest in new people and ideas. Both explanations refer to Zeffirelli's realistic style as the major attraction' (1987, pp. 83–4). The set was a crucial element, and 'the audience gasped when the curtain went up because it was all misty in this very-real looking Italian street and people were throwing out sheets to air; nothing as realistic had been seen for a very long time in Shakespeare' (Dench, 1996, p. 201). He made the costumes more casual than the usual elaborate Renaissance outfits and discarded traditional items like the wig used by many Romeos, so that John Stride could 'run his hand through his hair' in a natural gesture (Brown, 1969, p. 147). Unlike Gielgud, Zeffirelli insisted 'The verse must always have ... the rhythm of reality' and 'must never become music' (Zeffirelli, 1976, p. 440). He succeeded in this objective and '[t]he greatest innovations in this production lay in unifying words and stage business, and in making the actors' speech as lively and fluent as their physical action' (Brown, p. 184). But he paid a price insofar as he 'had no respect for the verse at all, and cut it appallingly ... for which he was rightly criticized' (Dench, p. 201). The production indeed elicited some hostile reviews, but these were countered by Kenneth Tynan's praise of it as 'revelatory and, perhaps, revolutionary' (Tynan, 1967, p. 49). It became 'one of the Old Vic's biggest successes after World War II', with a global tour that set attendance records in the United States, and earned a Tony award (Levenson, 1987, p. 104).

In the film Zeffirelli amplified some of his innovations, revised others, and took advantage of the medium in terms of setting, camera-work, and soundtrack. At the Old Vic, he had cast Judi Dench and John Stride, both 26 years old and trained verse speakers, as the lovers. For the movie he cast 16-year old Leonard Whiting and

15-year old Olivia Hussey (Zeffirelli, 1990, p. 244). The payoff was that 'Whiting and Hussey bring to their parts both innocence and exuberance that make the Capulet ball . . . and the balcony scenes believable moments of first-love excitement' (Willson, 2000, p. 182). The cost was that these actors could not successfully perform the demanding speeches or match the characterizations by John McEnery as Mercutio, Michael York as Tybalt, Pat Heywood as the Nurse, or Milo O'Shea as the Friar (Zeffirelli, 1990, p. 249). Juliet lost 'Gallop apace' and 'My dismal scene', but the cuts helped Hussey create a Juliet who is young, innocent, and delighted by her sexuality. Cuts also enhanced the innocence of Romeo, since they not only eliminated killing Paris but, as Deborah Cartmell notes, the scene where Romeo bribes the Apothecary (2000, p. 44). These choices contributed to the sense that the lovers were the victims of adults who are either clueless, like the Capulets, or sympathetic but maladroit, like the Nurse and the Friar.

Zeffirelli focused on scenes of dancing, fighting, and love-making. The Capulet ball is an event where adults provide an opportunity for the younger generation to release their energies apparently free from the feud, but Zeffirelli uses Tybalt to add disharmonies within the Capulet family to the conflict between families. Tybalt dances with Lady Capulet, who is attracted to him; and he realizes Romeo is wooing Juliet, so his challenge is motivated by an urgent threat to family honor. Even as Capulet tries to preserve harmony, his wife is flirting with his nephew and his daughter is falling in love with the son of his enemy.

These dissonances become the ground against which the harmony between Romeo and Juliet emerges, first in the staid dance in which Juliet is partnered by Paris and then in the wilder dance called for by Lady Capulet. This second dance reaches its climax when the outer circle of men and the inner circle of women whirl in opposite directions while the camera registers Juliet becoming motion-intoxicated. The dance is followed by a song entitled 'What is a youth?' which is performed by a young man as the guests listen in rapt stillness. While Jorgens calls it 'sickly sweet' (p. 82), the image of a young man's love as the fire that kindles the desire of a young woman articulates Zeffirelli's interpretation: for whereas the sonnet created by Romeo and Juliet foregrounds love's transcendence the song emphasizes its transience. The words also counterpoint the dialogue so that, as Patricia Tatspaugh notes, it is at 'So does the fairest maid' that

Romeo seizes Juliet's hand from behind a pillar (2000, p. 141). The melody wells up repeatedly during the rest of the film – in the balcony scene, at the moments of despair when each lover learns that Romeo is banished, at their farewell, during the potion scene, and during the scene in the tomb – until, finally, during the funeral procession, it becomes, in effect, an elegy for the lovers.

Zeffirelli not only has Romeo ascend to the balcony but uses the camera to share the lovers' intimacy. Juliet often speaks as Romeo is kissing her, so that when she proclaims 'the more I give to thee, / The more I have, for both are infinite' (2.1.177–8) she is articulating the desire they are enacting. And nothing makes Juliet seem so young, innocent, and exuberant as the giggle that bursts forth as Romeo kisses her – and that returns in their morning-after scene when Romeo leaps back into her arms. During Juliet's absence, as Romeo exclaims 'O blessed, blessed night', he expresses his euphoria by hanging from a branch of the tree he climbs to reach her, as he does when he runs down a hillside, leaping to touch branches on his way to ask the Friar to marry him to Juliet.

Another striking element is the way the fight echoes the dance, the way Mercutio's death echoes the Queen Mab segment, and the way Romeo's relation with Tybalt echoes his relation with Juliet: together these scenes embody the riddle posed by Romeo's 'Here's much to do with hate, but more with love.' On the way to the dance, Mercutio dons and doffs a death-mask before he bursts into the Queen Mab speech, and after the marriage of Romeo and Juliet he enters the frame wearing a handkerchief over his face so that the cloth forms a shroud-like mask. Whereas in the nighttime scene Mercutio appears with a torch flickering in front of his face, in this daytime scene he steps into the fountain in the square to escape the heat and, in effect, baptizes himself. The sexuality of the Queen Mab speech is echoed when Tybalt's insolence provokes Mercutio to announce 'Here is my fiddlestick' as his sword suddenly rises from the water. When Tybalt calls Romeo 'a villain', Romeo repeats his first contact with Juliet by seizing Tybalt's hand as he speaks of the love he bears his challenger. Tybalt pretends to be repulsed by the stench of Romeo's touch, washes his hand in the fountain, and provokes Mercutio by splashing water on him.

Like the first dance, the first fight is formal and contained as the young men encircle the combatants. This is the fight as performance, and their playfulness becomes explicit when Romeo's first attempt to stop them prompts Tybalt and Mercutio to stand side by side, point their blades at Romeo, and shake hands with mock-courtesy before they resume. As they fight, Tybalt manages to disarm Mercutio, puts the point of his blade at Mercutio's throat, and cuts off a lock of his hair; Mercutio disarms Tybalt, tosses him a wooden pitchfork, and mocks him by sharpening one sword on the other. As they close again, Romeo hurls Tybalt away, grabs Mercutio as he leaps down from the fountain, and pins his sword arm just as Tybalt's forward motion impales Mercutio. This scene echoes the Queen Mab scene, for just as Romeo takes Mercutio's head in his hands as he seeks to stop his collapse, so now Mercutio takes Romeo's head in his hands as he says 'I was hurt under your arm' (l. 103). Reversing the Queen Mab sequence, the camera isolates Mercutio as he staggers up the stairs, topples down, and dies – at which point Romeo seizes his friend's bloody handkerchief and, when he finds Tybalt, rubs his face with the bloodstained cloth.

This second fight is a wilder event, shot with a hand-held camera in a way that echoes the second dance. At the climax, Tybalt sends Romeo flying so that he lands on his back with his sword seemingly out of reach. Tybalt raises his weapons, runs forward – and stops, impaled by the sword we do not see Romeo raise. Tybalt stands in pre-carious equilibrium before he topples onto Romeo, who finds himself again embracing a Capulet whose hand he had taken moments earlier. Heaving off the body, he rises, cries 'O I am fortune's fool!' (l. 136), and seeks sanctuary with Friar, reversing his run from Juliet.

Whatever their limitations, Whiting and Hussey enable Zeffirelli to solve the tension inherent in the scenes in which the lovers collapse at the news Romeo is banished. From the nineteenth century onwards these scenes have proved difficult, especially for the actors playing Romeo. Even 18 years after this film, Martin Hoyle commented on how Kenneth Branagh, age 25, 'lay flat on the floor, bellowing bit-ter sobs like a child cheated of a promised treat' (*Financial Times,* 15 August, 1986; quoted by Loehlin, 2002, p. 186). However, when Hussey and Whiting collapse, their youth makes their responses seem a regression to a pre-adolescent state they have only recently left behind. Romeo also collapses in the tomb but the film pays a price for repeating this maneuver. In the Q2 text, Romeo's response to the news of Juliet's death and his final speech suggest he has undergone a transformation. Establishing such a contrast determines whether Romeo's suicide seems an act of transcendent love or, as happens here, the act of a helpless victim.

While Zeffirellii cut much from the Friar's long speeches in 2.2 and 3.3 and his final recapitulation, he added important non-verbal and verbal touches. In his first scene, the Friar resists Romeo's plea to perform the marriage and only after he sees a large cross in the church does he change his mind, apparently inspired by the idea that God will use the marriage to end the feud. Confronting Juliet's ultimatum, inspiration comes when he glances at the basket of flowers he was picking when Romeo met him. These moments testify to his faith but also prompt us to ask why his inspiration is not blessed with success. When Juliet refuses to leave the tomb, the Friar's cowardice is emphasized because he not only cries 'I dare no longer stay' (5.3.159) but repeats this cry three times as he flees. Since he also loses his final speech, he has no chance to receive absolution from the Prince, whose 'We still have known thee for a holy man' (l. 270) is also cut.

Zeffirelli's 120-line cut in the final scene also eliminates the speeches in which the heads of the two houses end the feud and promise to memorialize their children. Robert Stephens' Prince concludes by crying 'All are punished' (l. 295), and when he repeats that cry the last word echoes as if Verona itself is passing sentence on the older generation. The final couplet, spoken by Laurence Olivier as chorus, frames the shot in which the Capulets and Montagues exit in pairs following the bodies into the cathedral. At this point the melody of 'What is a Youth?' returns serving as an elegiac conclusion to the movie.

If Zeffirelli's film achieves some powerful effects often ignored by critics, it is also true that the weaknesses described by those critics are severe: 'the tragic scenes are heavily cut, perfunctory, and drowned in Rota's music'. Yet Loehlin concedes that 'the film overall conveys the exuberant youth and rich visual detail that made Zeffirelli's stage production such a landmark' (2000, p. 78). It was also an economic landmark: made for $2 million dollars, it grossed over $50 million world-wide (Crowl, 2008, p. 55). The film remains influential, and its availability on DVD and the Web insure it will continue to be the first performance seen by millions of viewers, who may see it before they read Shakespeare's play.

Baz Luhrmann, 1996

In *William Shakespeare's Romeo + Juliet*, Baz Luhrmann develops innovations from *West Side Story*, Bogdanov's production, and Zeffirelli's
film. Like *West Side Story*, Luhrmann translates the two houses into
racially composed gangs. Like Bogdanov, he makes the houses
part of a corrupt business world. In the way he creates a detailed
urban environment, uses the camera, composes the soundtrack,
and presents the lovers, Luhrmann both imitates and transforms
Zeffirelli's paradigm. Luhrmann also embodies a post-modern aes-
thetic, for if Zeffirelli's film seems visually and aurally saturated,
Luhrmann's increases that saturation by a whole order of magnitude,
in part through allusions to dozens of other movies and music videos
(Buhler, p. 91), and in part through editing. 'Luhrmann's film is the
most aggressively edited of all Shakespeare films, and it is in the editing room that his film finds its unique style and pace' (Crowl, p. 110).

That style and pace also come from the soundtrack Luhrmann created with music producer Nellee Hooper, music programmer Marius
DeVries, and arranger Craig Armstrong. When Kym Mazelle, singing
'Young Hearts Run Free', describes a marriage without love, she
seems to suggest Juliet's view of her mother and thus her motive for
falling in love with and proposing marriage to Romeo. When Des'ree
sings 'Kissing You', it counterpoints Romeo and Juliet's first glimpses
of one another and reaches its climax in the scene in which, echoing
Zeffirelli, Romeo hides behind a pillar, grabs Juliet's hand, and draws
her to him to begin their sonnet. A choir led by Quindon Tarver sings
'When Doves Cry' as Father Laurence decides to marry the lovers and
'Everybody's Free (to be Happy)' during the wedding.

It was also crucial to the film's success that while Luhrmann cast
young actors to play the lovers, he chose Leonardo DiCaprio, age
21, and Claire Danes, age 16, both of whom were already popular
with teenage audiences. A year later DiCaprio would star as another
doomed lover in *Titanic*, a movie which received the Best Picture
Oscar and became the highest grossing film of all time.

Luhrmann's film declares its allegiance to a post-modern aes-
thetic in the way it recreates the Chorus by interweaving theatrical,
televisual, and cinematic modes. It opens with an image of a television
set which gradually fills the film-screen as it goes from a blank screen

to one filled with static and then to a news program. As the phrase 'Star-Cross'd Lovers' appears, a newsreader delivers the first 12 lines of the Chorus while words and images flash by. 'Fair Verona' is introduced with shots of a skyline dominated by Capulet and Montague headquarters flanking a massive statue of Christ, and footage of a Verona Beach Police Department patrol car, providing a preview of the one institution that will attempt to sustain and the three that will destroy the lovers. Luhrmann also echoes the prologue's invocation of the stars as a choir sings 'O Verona', echoing the 'O Fortuna' which opens Carl Orff's *Carmina Burana* (Loehlin, 2000, p. 125). The prologue registers how the media reduce a theatrical classic to one in a series of tragic events that strut and fret their 15 minutes upon the screen even as the cinema presents what the newscast ignores. This prologue, moreover, in which 'there are no fewer than seventy separate edits in the sequence and many, many pans and zooms' (Buhler, p. 90), prepares the hermeneutic reflexes of the spectators to respond to the two hour's traffic of the screen.

The opening gunfight at the Phoenix gas station dances to the same hyperkinetic tempo. There are many small touches, such as close-ups which show guns engraved 'Sword 9mm series S', producing a modern version of Shakespeare's puns, as when Benvolio orders his comrades to 'put up your swords'. The scene comments on how Americans turn guns into fetishes when it shows an image of the Virgin Mary that adorns Tybalt's automatic, as if the feud could claim a religious blessing. In the fight itself 'we vicariously experience the intoxicating fun of violence, while being perfectly aware that this is a spectacle staged for our pleasure' (Loehlin, 2000, p. 126) – but we also register the discrepancy between the fun for the gangs and the cost to society. On the one hand, Tybalt proves to be the prince of marksmen, who first shoots Benvolio's gun out of his hand and then wounds Gregory in the arm when he could have killed him. On the other hand, where earlier he carefully grinds out a match, now in the heat of battle Tybalt hurls his cigarette into a trail of gasoline, touching off an explosion which turns the station to ashes – this Phoenix will *not* resurrect itself – and produces a fire, a traffic jam, and a scene of 'Riot police subduing looters, cars burning, shop windows smashed' (Pearce and Luhrmann, 1996, p. 15). The feud has the power to trigger violence that can barely be checked by the police who patrol this dystopia.

Even some critics who praised Luhrmann's densely allusive style point out it cannot hide the fact that the actors performing the younger generation 'speak with toneless naturalism, their reedy voices flattening out the elaborate poetic conceits of one of Shakespeare's most self-consciously verbal plays' (Loehlin, 2000, pp. 123–4). Luhrmann and Pearce diminished this problem by cutting much of the dialogue. Romeo and Juliet keep their sonnet-exchange and over half of the balcony dialogue. Danes loses her soliloquy while waiting for the Nurse, speaks only 12 lines of her epithalamium (3.1.20–32), only one line of her potion soliloquy, and five of her last eight lines to Romeo. Like Zeffirelli, Luhrmann preserves more of the first three than the last two acts: of the 29 chapters on the DVD, 23 present the first three acts while six present the last two acts and credits.

One striking element of Zeffirelli's film was the fountain in the town square in which Mercutio immerses himself, and Luhrmann makes water a key element of his production. As Gloria Capulet and the Nurse shout Juliet's name, the film cuts to '[t]he still, serene, submerged features of a beautiful young girl' (p. 32) who, by immersing herself in her bathtub, manages to insulate herself from the outside world. In a complementary scene, Romeo, having taken the drug offered by Mercutio during the Queen Mab speech and finding himself caught in a hallucinatory experience, soaks his head in a washbasin to help clear his mind – at which point he becomes enchanted by a tank filled with fish whose vivid yellows and blues reappear in the lovers' final scene. His wonder intensifies when he sees the face of a young woman who smiles at him with the radiance appropriate to her angelic costume. Extending this motif, Luhrmann uses a swimming pool in the Capulet garden to develop a variation on Zeffirelli's balcony scene. Romeo hears Juliet's monologue and surprises her when he says 'I take thee at thy word!' She turns abruptly, he reaches out to stabilize her, and they tumble into the pool. Although the screenplay prints the next two lines in which he promises to be new baptized, Romeo does not speak them, perhaps because their plunge into pool enacts the metaphor – a point emphasized when, after he defiantly shouts 'Thy kinsmen are no stop to me!' he must submerge to hide from a security guard. Water becomes the element that enables the lovers to hide from the feud yet express their desire in a scene so buoyant it seems they might float in the cup of life.

However, this sustaining element becomes stained by destructive events. The wedding chorus of 'Everybody's Free' is succeeded by the sound of gunfire and the sight of Mercutio shooting fish in the ocean. When Mercutio dies, a thunderstorm produces a downpour in which Romeo pursues and finally smashes into the car in which Tybalt has fled. When Tybalt points his gun at Romeo, Romeo, who does not attempt suicide later in Laurence's cell, presses the gun-barrel against his forehead screaming 'Or thou, or I, or both must go with him' three times. Unnerved, Tybalt backs away, stumbles, loses his gun, and tries to escape by climbing the stairs to the fountain – at which point Romeo fires five shots that send his body plunging into the basin, where his blood begins to incarnadine the water. When Romeo drops the gun, rain splashes on the image of the Virgin as if she were being purified. It is this rain-soaked Romeo who enters Juliet's room to complete their marriage, and the next morning, as the camera gazes down at the serenely sleeping couple, it is a flashback to Tybalt's corpse that wakes Romeo. When Romeo immerses himself in the swimming pool, he mouths a silent 'Adieu' in an image which echoes how they first saw each other.

For Romeo, to be with Juliet is to live in a world sustained by water, and to be exiled is to live in a desert, since Mantua proves to be a trailer park in a dusty wasteland. When, hearing of her death, Romeo cries 'Then I defy you stars!' he is facing a blazing sun which presides over this arid landscape. This scene contrasts with the lovers' reunion in the cathedral, as Romeo – having bought the poison the apothecary keeps 'inside a statue-of-Our-Lady table lamp' (p. 148) – finds Juliet illuminated by the yellow light of hundreds of candles and the blue light of dozens of neon crosses which create 'a shimmering aquatic glow, as if Romeo and Juliet were indeed underwater' (Loehlin, 2000, p. 129).

This scene proves to be an agonizing version of the ending, in which Luhrmann echoes Garrick's innovation. Juliet tenderly touches Romeo's cheek just as he finishes swallowing the poison and Romeo, abruptly dropping the vial, realizes that he has acted under a tragic misapprehension and that a split-second might have saved his life. Juliet, in turn, realizes that, due to a disastrous mischance, her touch has come a split-second too late. She addresses 'Thy lips are warm' to a husband who is alive and when Romeo whispers 'Thus with a kiss

I die' a tear continues to slide down his cheek after he stops breathing. With Romeo dead and the Friar omitted, we endure the process by which Juliet cocks the hammer and pulls the trigger of Romeo's automatic – and the camera cuts to 'the two young lovers at peace, lying together in the deathbed' (p. 160) just as they slept after consummating their marriage. The effect is 'the combined illusion . . . that they know what we know and we feel what they feel' (Buhler, p. 93).

Luhrmann proceeds to close his frame in reverse order. He cuts to Captain Prince's twice-uttered 'All are punished!' while the grieving parents stand under umbrellas to watch the bodies being loaded into an ambulance. The news reader recites the Prince's final speech and prepares to move on, her use of the superlative simply a ploy applied to one sensational tragedy after another. The picture disappears, the television screen fills with static and then goes black as it shrinks in size. As the credits roll, Radiohead performs 'Exit Music (for a Film)' in which the singer seems to speak as one of the lovers, describing how they will escape this world, find peace in another world, and curse all those who proved so inhospitable their love. His words also seem to echo Mercutio's curse and thus suggest that only the spectators might learn to prevent hate destroying love in their world.

Conclusion

Watching a film of *Romeo and Juliet* will illuminate how the words can be translated into action, but doing so can also suggest that what you have seen is *the* way to perform the text – another reason to watch a second film. In addition to the films, there are a number of audio recordings which present something very close to a full text of the play. After watching Zeffirelli's or Luhrmann's film, both of which omit Juliet's soliloquy in 4.3, it is illuminating to hear Claire Bloom's performance, with its breathtaking projection of the path Juliet takes in order to prompt herself to drink the potion. In addition, there are recordings by Ellen Terry, Samantha Bond, Kate Beckinsale, and Maria Miles that offer different phrasings of this speech. As you listen to one or more of them, you can also imagine how Juliet handles the vial, how she drinks the potion, how she loses consciousness – actions which will arouse strong visceral responses in a theater audience. You can repeat this process with any segment or scene. By engaging in such explorations, you will be primed to catch the nuances of the next performance you witness, and take another step in a recursive process that will enrich your future readings and discussions of the play.

6   Critical Assessment

Romeo and Juliet remains one of the most popular plays in the theater and, with an irony Shakespeare might well appreciate, the title figures have become at least as famous as the patterns of doomed love mockingly cited by Mercutio (2.3.37–42). A number of critics have praised the play as a superlative achievement. T.J.B. Spencer, for example, announces that '[n]othing in European drama had hitherto achieved the organization of so much human experience when Shakespeare, at about the age of thirty, undertook the story of Romeo and Juliet' (1967, p. 7). Kenneth Muir claims that '[i]n his last scene [Shakespeare] wrote the finest poetry which had yet been heard on the English stage; . . . and in the characters of Mercutio and the Nurse he displayed for the first time his unequalled power for the dramatic presentation of character' (1978, p. 46). And Cedric Watts asserts that 'at the time of its appearance, *Romeo and Juliet* was the most brilliant tragedy to have emerged since the ancient Greek drama', adding that '[i]t was wholly original in making the central matter the combined fates of two young lovers within a credibly diversified modern society and in telling their story with such acumen and stylistic verve' (1991, p. 3).

The comic dimension: The Nurse, Friar Laurence, and Mercutio

Romeo and Juliet is striking for its mixture of comic and tragic elements, and the comedy is crucial to the play's theatrical success. The Nurse, the Friar, and Mercutio not only provide much of the comic energy but also articulate contrasting points of view that comment on and, in turn, are commented on by the speech and action of the lovers; and they function as key agents in the plot, for after the Nurse and the Friar arrange the marriage, the actions of the trio, along with Capulet's insistence on accelerating Juliet's marriage to Paris, help precipitate the play's tragic conclusion.

In his 1765 edition of Shakespeare, Samuel Johnson wrote that the Nurse 'is one of the characters in which the Author delighted: he has, with great subtilty [*sic*] of distinction, drawn her at once loquacious and secret, obsequious and insolent, trusty and dishonest' (VIII, p. 957). Her comic energies emerge immediately during her famous monologue (1.3.14–64). 'How Shakespeare came to invent the extraordinary blank verse he gives her is a mystery', as Hibbard writes (1981, p. 125; see Commentary for 1.3.11–64), and Watts observes that in creating the Nurse 'Shakespeare has learnt the cogency of the apparently digressive, the relevance of the seemingly irrelevant' (p. 85). Besides insisting on how young Juliet is, the primary effect of this speech is to present an image of Juliet's transition from infancy to childhood at the very moment she is about to move from childhood to adolescence (Dalsimer, 1986, p. 86). The Nurse's bawdy, as Sasha Roberts notes, differs from the bawdy of Sampson, Gregory, and Mercutio. First, the Nurse 'does not associate sex with violence but rather with mutual pleasure, moreover she emphasizes women as the subject (not objects) of sexual pleasure' (1998, p. 90). Second, 'by contrast to much of the bawdy talk of male servants and gentlemen, the focus of the Nurse's bawdy is rarely upon male or female genitalia but rather upon the *act* of making love' (p. 90). Third, her bawdy 'counters the romantic idealization of Juliet – instead the Nurse emphasizes her sexuality and the physicality of her desire – and consequently it challenges, even undermines the idealization of romantic love in the play' (p. 90). Although Roberts does not say so, her analysis suggests that Juliet's surrogate mother has instilled a sense of female agency in choosing a partner and a belief that in making love such partners can create mutual pleasure. That attitude is announced in the Nurse's scene-concluding speech, in which she exhorts Juliet to 'seek happy nights to happy days' (1.3.107). This belief may also help explain the logic which leads her to betray Juliet: the Nurse, it would seem, decides she must wean Juliet from Romeo so that she can enter a marriage approved by her parents and in which happy nights will indeed produce happy days.

In terms of the dramatic design, the Nurse is a classic figure of romantic comedy, since she is a servant who conspires with her mistress so that she can marry the young man she loves rather than the man chosen by her parents. Indeed, when the Friar exits to marry the lovers the play lacks only the scene where the father accepts that he has been outwitted, blesses the couple, and joins in the celebration. Even as the plot turns tragic and Capulet's threats persuade the Nurse to betray Juliet (3.5. 204–34), when she tries to wake Juliet for the wedding (4.4.1–12) she continues to address her by her pet names and make the same jokes she made when helping her prepare for her night with Romeo. Here, what was once comic becomes pathetic, underlining how Juliet has cut her off and the shock that awaits her before she disappears from the play.

G.B. Evans notes that '[c]ritical reaction to Friar Lawrence ranges from the uneasily ambiguous to the downright hostile' (2003, p. 23), and suggests these responses are prompted by the way that 'Shakespeare . . . creates a character in which the Friar's function as orthodox moral commentator . . . seems to be at odds with aspects of his character and actions as a man' (p. 25). Critics often speak of the Friar as a choral figure, and during his opening speech he offers a frame that differs from the image of the lovers as 'star-crossed': instead, he explains that just as a single plant may have lethal and life-saving properties so human nature is split between self-destructive 'rude will' and soul-saving 'grace' (2.2.23–31). He articulates a vision of a world governed by a benign providence, and completes the articulation of the three codes – honor, justice, and Christianity – that create the dilemma which entraps Romeo in 3.1. His lecture on plants also foreshadows the potion he creates to preserve Juliet's life and the poison Romeo buys to end his life.

With the entrance of Romeo, the Friar takes up the roles of surrogate father and benign practicer in arranging the clandestine marriage. It is in his role as surrogate father that he becomes a source of comedy, teasing Romeo for doting on and then forgetting Rosaline, and his 'Holy Saint Francis, what a change is here' (l. 65) reliably provokes laughter. The Friar is essential not only because he can marry the lovers but because he agrees to perform the marriage as the means to transform private romance into public reconciliation. In the scene that completes the second act (2.5), the Friar succeeds in producing the classic conclusion to a romantic comedy when he marries the lovers, and if the play were such a comedy then he, like Friar Francis in *Much Ado about Nothing*, would be applauded for his benign practice. This highpoint is followed by the scene in which

Romeo obeys the Christian command to turn the other cheek in the
face of Tybalt's provocations (3.1.60–71), invokes justice as he tries to
persuade Mercutio and Tybalt to break off their fight (ll. 86–7), and,
having contributed to Mercutio's death, achieves revenge by killing
Tybalt (ll. 109–15). In the scenes that follow, Friar Laurence performs
in ways that display his own mixture of grace and rude will. For
example, not only does he (or in Q1, the Nurse) thwart Romeo's suicide attempt but he enables Romeo to regain his adult self-control.
Because he decides to delay revealing the marriage (3.3.149–53), however, he also contributes to Juliet's tragic dilemma and, in response to
her suicide threat, devises a plan which proves fatal to Paris, Romeo,
and Juliet. In the final scene, moreover, he abandons Juliet, leaving
her free to commit suicide. Brought before the Prince, he acknowledges his guilt, and declares himself ready to be executed – only to
have the Prince declare 'We still have known thee for a holy man'
(5.3.266–71). Critics who see the play as celebrating the transcendent love of Romeo and Juliet tend to follow the Prince in defending
the Friar as a holy man who contributes to ending the feud. Other
critics, however, see his cowardice as the culmination of a series of
reckless choices. 'In a sense, then, what began as a potential work
of "grace" . . . is twisted instead by the Friar's choice of "desperate"
means, into something verging on a work of "rude will" . . . Ironically,
Friar Lawrence [sic] illustrates through his own actions the moral dan-
gers inherent in man's dual nature that he had warned against in his
opening choral speech' (Evans, 2003, pp. 24–5).

Mercutio provides an especially vivid demonstration of Shakespeare's power of invention, for whereas the Nurse in Brooke's poem
is already a substantial figure, Mercutio exists in a single, brief passage (ll. 252–90; see the excerpt in Sources). Shakespeare, however,
transforms him into a character so vibrant that, as Johnson remarked,
'Mercutio's wit, gaiety, and courage, will always procure him friends
who wish him a longer life' (VIII, pp. 956–7). Johnson's praise is
echoed by many subsequent writers, as Joseph A. Porter indicates in
Shakespeare's Mercutio: His History and Drama:

> As is well known, Mercutio is a landmark in Shakespeare's early devel-
> opment of characterization in distinctive speech, and much of the
> impressionistic admiration (as well as some disapproval) he has elicited
> has been for his speech. Harbage (*Reader's Guide*, p. 145) speaks of 'his

matchless exercise in verbal cameo-cutting and imaginative fooling,' Holland ('Shakespeare's Mercutio,' pp. 118–9) of his 'puns, rhymes, jokes, set-speeches and other masks,' and Snyder ('*Romeo*,' p. 395) of the fact that 'speech for him is a constant play on multiple possibilities: puns abound because two or three meanings are more fun than one.'   (1988, p. 99)

In adding that Mercutio seems to stand 'outside the main plot' (p. 99), Porter points toward caveats expressed by critics from John Dryden onward, who claim Shakespeare erred by creating a figure who threatens to overshadow Romeo. Those who subscribe to this view suggest that the creator was so delighted with his creature that he let Mercutio dominate scenes even when this subverted the design – most notably in the Queen Mab speech, perceived as 'a brilliant *tour de force* of doubtful dramatic or thematic relevance' (G.B. Evans, 2003, p. 21). Like the Nurse, Mercutio is one of the main exponents of sexual commentary, although his bawdy, as Roberts notes, focuses on genitalia, equates love with violence, and reduces women to objects used to satisfy male appetite. The fact that Mercutio is blind to the positive potential of heterosexual love helps to underline what is so valuable about the love of Romeo and Juliet.

Contrasting evaluations of Mercutio come into focus in the way that critics respond to his belief that he must challenge Tybalt to restore the honor Romeo seems to have abandoned. Porter claims that '[a]s ready as Tybalt to take offense, Mercutio seems more admirable inasmuch as the honor he dies defending is a friend's rather than his own' (p. 102). Other critics, however, contend that since Mercutio is not a party to the feud, and since Benvolio apparently feels no need to defend his kinsman's honor, Mercutio 'was simply meddling where he should not have been, and Romeo's willingness to avenge his death was more a reflection on Romeo's own magnanimity than on Mercutio's worth to him' (Wright, 1997, p. 75). Of the supporting roles, Mercutio offers the most powerful mixture of comic and tragic elements, and 'Mercutio continues to be the wild card of the play, the role which, when one goes to the theatre, one can least predict or anticipate' (Wright, p. 195).

Finally, while some critics perceive that the partial visions of love articulated by the Nurse and Mercutio ultimately serve to confirm the transcendent nature of the passion of Juliet and her Romeo, for others their critiques help insure that our sympathy for the lovers does not blind us to the fact that they are adolescents who, however extraordinary their love and, in particular, the language in which they create that love, make choices which contribute to their doom. This points to what is probably the most contested critical issue, namely whether the play succeeds or fails as a tragedy.

Is *Romeo and Juliet* a successful tragedy?

F. E. Halliday notes that '*Romeo and Juliet* is remarkable in being an Elizabethan tragedy . . . without a villain' in which 'disaster is brought about by circumstance or fate, so that it might almost be called "The Tragedy of Errors" ' (1964, p. 89), and this alternate title sums up the charge made by those who believe that a plot pervaded by accident undermines the sense of inevitability necessary to create a successful tragedy. G.K. Hunter highlights another problem, namely that 'The rash and personal passion of Romeo and Juliet can hardly claim a truly tragic significance if it cannot be caught up in the corporate and continuing life of Verona' (1974, p. 8). Examining the debate illuminates these tensions in the design and exemplifies some major developments in critical approaches to this play.

In his famous and frequently republished *Shakespearean Tragedy* (1904), A.C. Bradley develops premises which provide a starting point for a critique of *Romeo and Juliet*. Bradley assumes there is a 'substance' of Shakespearean tragedy, and claims this substance is fully realized in *Hamlet*, *Othello*, *King Lear*, and *Macbeth*. He asserts that '*Romeo and Juliet* . . . is a pure tragedy, but it is an early work, and in some respects an immature one' (p. xlviii) and specifies the ways in which the play seems immature. Each of the four great tragic heroes, he argues, is 'an exceptional being', not only because he possess a 'high degree of public importance' but because his nature 'raises him in some respect much above the average level of humanity' (p. 12). Each hero also displays 'a fatal tendency to identify the whole being with one interest, object, passion, or habit of mind' (p. 12) which is in conflict with other fundamental values, creating the type of struggle exemplified by Hamlet's effort to achieve revenge although revenge is incompatible with state justice and Christian mercy. Bradley adds that 'we find that it is in . . . the maturest works, that this inward struggle is most emphasized' and that *Romeo and Juliet* is among the plays 'where the hero contends with an outward force but comparatively little with himself' (p. 11). When Shakespeare wrote this play, moreover, he had not yet developed the pattern in which 'The center of the tragedy . . . may be said with equal truth to lie in action issuing from character, or in character issuing in action' (p. 20). Bradley also points out that 'any *large* admission of chance into the tragic sequence would certainly weaken, and might destroy, the sense of causal connection of character, deed, and catastrophe' (p. 8). While privileging the essential elements of the major tragedies enabled Bradley to produce much excellent criticism, it also supported the presumption that any Shakespearean tragedy which lacked one or more of these elements would be only a partial success.

In his study of *Shakespearian Tragedy* (1948), H.B. Charlton, who declares himself 'a devout Bradleyite' (p. 4), builds on Bradley's analysis, although he, too, thinks *Romeo and Juliet* fails as a tragedy. For Charlton, the four great tragedies demonstrate that the form depends on a sense of universality, a sense of momentousness, and a sense that the destruction of the tragic hero is inevitable. After showing that *Titus Andronicus, Richard III*, and *Richard II* never integrate these elements, Charlton suggests that when Shakespeare came to write *Romeo and Juliet* he conducted an experiment by 'casting in fresh directions to find the universality, the momentousness, and above all the inevitability of all-compelling tragedy' (p. 51). He turned from the fall of princes to an Italian story of romantic love, but this choice itself presented challenges since 'Romeo and Juliet were . . . just a boy and a girl in a novel; and as such they had no claim to the world's attention except through their passion and their fate' (p. 51). The focus on love leading to marriage might seem to fulfill the criterion of universality, but embodying such love in young people of no high station made it difficult to produce the other two elements. That Shakespeare sought to create a sense of inevitability is clear from the first Chorus: '[t]he feud is to provide the sense of immediate, Fate that of ultimate inevitability' (p. 52). The feud, however, fails to elicit a sense of inevitability because it is not dramatized as a force equal to the love of Romeo and Juliet. Thus '[i]f the tragedy is to march relentlessly to its end, leaving no flaw in the sense of inevitability . . . it clearly must depend for that indispensable tragic impression . . . on its scattered suggestions of doom and of malignant fate'. But '[i]n a Christian, rather than a pagan world, Fate was no longer a deity strong enough to carry the responsibility of a tragic universe; at most, it could intervene causally as pure luck, and bad luck as a motive turns tragedy to mere chance' (p. 61). In a move repeated by some later critics, Charlton claims it is the poetry which makes the play successful in spite of these defects: 'Shakespeare has but conquered us by a trick; the experiment carries him no nearer to the heart of tragedy' (p. 63).

In *Shakespeare's World of Images* (1949), Donald A. Stauffer argues that if the play is a tragedy of fate then Romeo and Juliet must be seen as 'puppets' (p. 55) before he reformulates the problem of the play's design:

> On the surface, social evil is castigated and purged by 'Fate,' which is an extra-human moral order. Yet in contrast to this often declared thesis, and by no means reconciled with it, Shakespeare intrudes a line of thinking which is to become central in his serious philosophy: that the causes of tragedy lie in the sufferers themselves. The doctrines of individual responsibility and of fate as a social Nemesis offer divergent motivations: this play may fail as a serious tragedy because Shakespeare blurs the focus and never makes up his mind entirely as to who is being punished, and for what reason.   (pp. 55–6)

The influence of the critique developed by Bradley, Charlton and Stauffer is registered in G.I. Duthie's Cambridge edition (1955), where he declares that the play fails as a tragedy of fate because, as Charlton argues, Shakespeare was so much more interested in the lovers than in the feud that the disaster seems 'a matter of sheer bad luck' (p. xxvii); and that it fails as a tragedy of character because, as Stauffer argues, while the lovers are rash their flaws are not the primary cause of their destruction. 'What we actually have then is a drama of Fate involving the destruction of two innocent victims who have defects of character which are not properly worked into the pattern' (p. xxxi).

A number of scholars responded to this critique by seeking to demonstrate that the play succeeds as a medieval tragedy of fortune, as a tragedy which synthesizes love and hate through fate, or as a tragedy of fate.

John Lawlor (1961), for example, argues that the play develops from the medieval form of tragedy in which 'Fortune knows nothing of human deserving' but 'her activities are not, in the end, inscrutable; for those who are minded to learn, a greater good is in prospect' (p. 124). On Lawlor's account, Shakespeare began to develop this kind of tragedy in the deposition and death of Richard II, where he stages events which point 'to . . . the recognition of a greater good . . . placing it beyond the bounds of life [on earth]' (pp. 129–30), and emphasizes that this good can be achieved when 'death has a sacrificial quality' (p. 130). *Romeo and Juliet* presents an action in which the tragic figures achieve this greater good through self-sacrifice: '[t]hat Death has no final power over the lovers is the great truth to which we are directed by their own rapturous hyperboles and by the central fact of their love, its freedom from any taint of the merely clandestine' (p. 138). He presents a different perception of the nature of this tragedy:

> What we see at the close of *Romeo and Juliet* is not simply a renewal of a pattern disturbed, but its re-ordering; life is not continued merely; it is regenerated. Only thus do we experience the quality of 'Beauty too rich for use, for earth too dear'. It is earth, the realm of Fortune, that is the loser . . . so this love is placed, fittingly, at once beyond reach and beyond change.
> (p. 127)

Lawlor concludes that '[i]f we can lay aside our preconceived notions alike of the "tragedy of character" and "tragedy of fortune" we may see that *Romeo and Juliet* is profoundly consistent with the longer run of the Shakespearian imagination' (pp. 142–3).

In *Not Wisely But Too Well: Shakespeare's Love Tragedies* (1957), Franklin M. Dickey distinguishes not two but three different forces generating the tragic outcome:

> On the one hand it can be demonstrated that the catastrophe develops from faults of character: Romeo's impetuous nature leads him to despair and die. On the other hand the text also gives us reason to believe that the love of Romeo and Juliet comes to a terrible end because of the hatred between the two families. And yet a third view makes fate the main cause of the final disaster: Romeo and Juliet had to die because they were star-cross'd.
> (pp. 63–4)

He argues that love, hate, and fate combine to produce a unified work of art so that '[j]udged by Elizabethan standards, the play is . . . a carefully wrought tragedy which balances hatred against love and which makes fortune the agent of divine justice without absolving anyone from his responsibility for the tragic conclusion' (p. 64). The play presents hatred as a civic issue: 'Hatred . . . was of particular concern to magistrates because the well-being of any state depended upon the mutual affection of its citizens.... Both the political and ethical consequences of hatred are explored in *Romeo and Juliet*' (p. 96). In exercising his free will, Romeo precipitates the tragic event and he is thus 'like Othello in that he is responsible for his own chain of passionate actions' (p. 114) – actions that begin when he kills Tybalt and continue in the choices that follow. 'Shakespeare is careful to make Romeo guilty of sinful action under the influence of passion, while at the same time making us sympathize with Romeo's agonies of despair.... Romeo's last passion-driven act is to kill himself just before Juliet awakes, and her suicide may be thought of as a direct result of his' (pp. 115–16). Finally, he suggests the Prince's closing speeches articulate the play's tragic pattern in a comprehensive fashion:

> When we look back over the course of the hatred, we see the truth of Escalus's sentence, 'All are punish'd.' Fate has worked to produce an evenhanded justice. The force of Mercutio's dying imprecation on both houses appears at the end of the tragedy in the mysterious death of Lady Montague on the night of her son's suicide. Her death, Shakespeare's addition to his source as are the deaths of Paris and Mercutio, evens the score between the families. Partisan pays for partisan and kinsman for kinsman.... It is precise and ironical justice that quenches the one passion by means of its opposite. *Romeo and Juliet*, no less than Shakespeare mature tragedies, celebrates the great vision of order by which the English Renaissance still lives.   (p. 101)

In *Shakespeare's Tragic Practice* (1979), Bertrand Evans analyzes *Romeo and Juliet* as a play shaped by 'Fate as Practiser':

> More than any other of Shakespeare's, not even excepting *Othello*, *Romeo and Juliet* is a tragedy of unawareness; and more than any other of Shakespeare's, not even excepting *Macbeth*, it is a tragedy of Fate. Fate is the controlling practiser, and the entire action of the play represents her at work in the details of her housekeeping.... The Prologue ... notifies us of two essential facts: that the lovers' deaths will be the means by which Fate ends the feud of the rival households, and that the details of Fate's progress to that end will constitute the very action of the play.   (pp. 22–3)

Evans develops his analysis as relentlessly as the Fate he claims supervises the action, arguing that *every* choice made by the *dramatis personae* helps produce the predestined end. Indeed, he argues that Fate and the action begin simultaneously, for '[t]hough the lovers have not yet met or, presumably, heard of each other, the pattern of their destruction is begun with Sampson's thumb-biting' (p. 24). After the Prince issues his ultimatum, Evans asserts that 'thanks to the Prologue . . . we can recognize that all the persons we have so far seen . . . have unknowingly acted out the first movement in Fate's tragedy' (p. 24). He claims that by the time the Prince banishes Romeo we have witnessed a chain of events so inexorable that '[b]ut for that thumb-biting servant, Romeo would now be a free man' (p. 34). Evans also claims that since 'it would be preposterous to suppose that the dramatist means Fate to occupy a lower level of awareness than our own we are obliged to suspect that Fate is malign and aware rather than benign but unaware' (p. 32). Although Evans does not say so, spectators who perceive Fate as malignant will confront a challenge when the Friar tells Juliet that 'A greater power than we can contradict . . . Hath thwarted our intent' (5.3.153–4). Since he must be thinking of the Christian god, either Fate is the 'greater power' or Fate is God's agent, prompting the question whether God also is malign. Finally, Evans claims that an omnipresent sense of the characters' unawareness is the means to insure that audiences never forget that '[o]ver the unnaturally bright and shining first balcony scene . . . the Prologue's doom casts an oppressive shadow' (p. 29). While the action of this scene occurs in a place shadowed by the risk of death, the lovers may create an incandescent joy that renders the shadow invisible.

Critics who describe the play as a failed tragedy sometimes attribute that failure in part to the prominence of comic characters whom they perceive as not fully integrated into the tragic action. Looking at *The Comic Matrix of Shakespeare's Tragedies* (1979), Susan Snyder analyzes the play as an experiment in which comedy is an integral element:

> The movement of *Romeo and Juliet* is unlike that of any other Shakespearean tragedy. It becomes, rather than is, tragic. Other tragedies have reversals, but here the reversal is so complete as to constitute a change of genre. Action and characters begin in the familiar comic mold and are then transformed, or discarded, to compose the shape of tragedy. . . . isolating [this aspect of the design] can reveal a good deal about *Romeo*, and may suggest why this early experimental tragedy has seemed to many to fall short of full tragic effect.   (p. 57)

Snyder shows how Shakespeare employed his skill in composing romantic comedy to create a romantic tragedy in which Mercutio's death produces a pivot from one genre to another:

> Comedy is organized like a game. The ascendency goes to the clever ones who can take advantage of sudden openings, plot strategies, and adapt flexibly to an unexpected move. But luck and instinct win games as well as skill, and comedy takes account of the erratic laws of chance . . . and, more basically, of the instinctive attunement to underlying pattern that crowns lovers . . . with final success. Romeo and Juliet, young and in love and defiant of obstacles, are attuned to the basic movement of the comic game toward social regeneration.   (pp. 58–9)

This objective seems attainable since '[t]he feud itself seems more a matter of mechanical reflex than of deeply felt hatred' (p. 59); and the threat posed by Tybalt seems manageable since '[w]hile he is alive, Tybalt is an alien' to the comic energies (p. 60). The pivot occurs in Mercutio's abrupt death, where 'Shakespeare makes the birth of tragedy coincide exactly with the symbolic death of comedy' (p. 62). Romeo's ability to evade the feud ceases when he realizes that 'he *must* kill Tybalt, he *must* run away, he is Fortune's fool' (p. 62). In addition, while the Friar and Nurse are not killed, they 'sharpen the tragedy by their failure to find a part in the dramatic progress' (p. 65). Against Bradley's claim that '[t]he center of the tragedy . . . may be said . . . to lie in action issuing from character, or in character issuing in action' (p. 20), Snyder argues that the dramatist created 'an ironic dissociation of character from the direction of events' (p. 70). Snyder also notes that the play 'locates this extraordinariness not so much in the two youthful lovers as in the love itself' (pp. 67–8), adding 'To stress milieu in this way is necessarily to down-grade the importance of individual temperament and motivation . . . In this unusual Shakespearean tragedy, it is not what you are that counts, but the world you live in' (p. 70).

In *Man's Estate: Masculine Identity in Shakespeare* (1981), Coppélia Kahn explores how the patriarchal society represented in Shakespeare's plays enacts the rites of passage undergone by adolescents; and how, in the histories and tragedies, this patriarchal order thwarts young men from forming the secure identities and stable relations necessary for marriage and children. Shakespeare composed the first two acts as if the play were to be a comedy in which '[g]rowing up requires that [young men and women] separate themselves from their parents by forming an intimate bond that supersedes filial bonds, a bond with a person of the opposite sex' (p. 83). Rejecting the idea that the play is a tragedy of errors, she proposes that the feud is an integral element in this society and central to the action in precisely the way Charlton believed necessary to create a sense of tragic inevitability:

> the feud in a realistic social sense is the primary tragic force in the play – not the feud as an agent of fate but the feud as an extreme and peculiar expression of patriarchal society . . . The feud is the deadly *rite de passage* that promotes masculinity at the price of life. Undeniably, the feud is bound up with a pervasive sense of *fatedness*, but that sense finds its objective correlative in the dynamics of the feud and of the society in which it is embedded.
> (p. 84)

For Kahn, the play prompts us to ask not only 'What's in a name?' but also 'What's in a feud?' The answer to 'What's in a feud?' is that it inscribes in the children of each house a hatred which, although culturally created, is experienced as natural, hence inescapable:

> For the sons and daughters of Verona, the feud constitutes socialization into patriarchal norms in two ways. First, it reinforces their identities as sons and daughters by allying them with their paternal household against another paternal household, thus polarizing all social relations, particularly their marital choices, in terms of filial allegiance. . . . Second, the feud . . . leads them to scorn women and to associate them with effeminacy and emasculation, while it links sexual intercourse with aggression and violence against women, rather than with pleasure and love.   (p. 86)

Romeo and Juliet seek to evade the imperatives encoded in their names when Friar Laurence marries them; and when Romeo, encounters Tybalt, he seeks to evade the latter's challenge until the death of Mercutio 'poses the two conflicting definitions of manhood between which Romeo must make his tragic choice' (pp. 86–7). Mercutio's decision to challenge Tybalt 'though he is neither Montague nor Capulet suggests that feuding has become the normal social pursuit for young men in Verona' (p. 90). Only Romeo and Paris attempt to form a relation leading to marriage, and they present a contrast between romantic love and an arranged marriage as the path to creating such a new family.

The heroine's situation is even more restricted since 'Juliet's growing up is hastened and intensified by having to resist the marriage arranged for her by her father.' The effect of this pressure is that 'Verona's daughters have, in effect, no adolescence, no sanctioned period of experiment with adult identities or activities' (p. 93). Juliet's mother asks her if she can 'like of Paris' love' (1.3.98), without telling her that Capulet has suggested a two-year engagement, and Juliet proposes to Romeo that night (p. 97). The next day, when she responds to the Nurse's 'Shame come to Romeo', Juliet learns that 'Romeo's "name" in the sense of his identity as well as his reputation now rests not on his loyalty to the Montagues but on Juliet's loyalty to him and their reciprocal identities as husband and wife apart from either house' (p. 98). While the fight between Romeo and Paris may seem a tragic error, it embodies the remorseless logic of the feud since even the two young men who have sought to define themselves as lovers end up fighting to the death (p. 90). In the last scene Kahn concludes that their 'love-death . . . is the lovers' triumphant assertion over the impoverished and destructive world that has kept them apart' (p. 103).

In 'Ideology and the Feud' (1996), Susan Snyder develops her earlier insight that the play 'locates this [tragic] extraordinariness not so much in the two youthful lovers as in the love itself' (pp. 67–8). Where Kahn sees the feud as 'an extreme and peculiar expression of patriarchal society', Snyder argues that '[t]he dramatic *expression* of dynastic hostility may seem extreme and eccentric, but the feud in its operations acts like any ideology, indeed offers a model of how ideology works' (p. 88). Shakespeare did not have our modern (and conflicting) formulations of 'ideology', but he composed a play which presents ideology in the experience of the characters:

> The feud operates in the classic way of language and of ideology: it creates meaning by differentiating. . . . Capulets define who they are against Montagues, Montagues against Capulets. 'This' can only be distinguished when set against 'that', however arbitrary such distinctions are in language and other social constructions. The feud is not a matter of contrary ideas, not a matter of ideas at all, but of repeated, habitual actions that keep reasserting the defining distinctions between 'us' and 'them'.   (pp. 90–1)

The feud seems not to be operating when the lovers meet 'unlabelled, as a faceless youth and an anonymous girl at a party' (p. 89), free to act outside its constraints; and even when they discover each other's names their passion prompts them to believe they can escape the strictures of family identity. Thus '[t]he news that Mercutio is dead completes Romeo's total absorption into the avenger-role prescribed for him in the code of honour, the role from which he had earlier distanced himself so carefully' (p. 94). And having married Romeo, Juliet becomes a traitor to her family and, although they are unaware of the marriage, her family in effect excommunicates her for becoming a Montague (p. 95).

This analysis also prompts Snyder to challenge the claim that in willing themselves to commit suicide the lovers manage to achieve a transcendent love:

> Enclosed by Veronese social formations, they do not rise above so much as withdraw inward. Romeo and Juliet have no space of their own. (p. 92) . . .
>
> Instead, the play's physical dimensions only confirm that 'there is no world without Verona walls' (3.3.17). Verona, constituted by the feud, asserts itself like any ideology as the only reality there is.   (p. 93)

She argues that, seen in terms of ideology, the play presents a form of inevitability more powerful than anything Charlton thought necessary for successful tragedy:

> The lovers' death looks avoidable on the plot level, a matter of misunderstanding and bad timing, but from this perspective the tragic finale inside the family tomb . . . is all too inevitable. I have been arguing that . . . the norms [of society] themselves bring about the tragedy. One could go further and propose that the tragic predicament – possibilities for human development narrowed down and cut off – is built into the operations of ideology.   (p. 95)

Her reading suggests that the play does not present a tragedy created by a misaligned social organization but rather represents the truth that *any* social organization, by its very nature as a social organization, will render the lives of its subjects potentially tragic. Snyder answers Charlton's critique by claiming not only that the play is thoroughly tragic but that it teaches us to recognize the potentially tragic nature of our own lives.

Conclusion

The history of the play recounted in these last three chapters suggests that at the heart of *Romeo and Juliet* is an enduring tension between the love story and the feud such that in many productions as one element is emphasized the other recedes. At one end of the spectrum, when Romeo and Juliet are played by charismatic actors, the performance can magnify the lovers and diminish the feud, especially if Romeo does not encounter and kill Paris in the final scene. In these productions, their love becomes a force that not only enables Romeo and Juliet to transcend death but compels their parents to redeem their children's scapegoat-like sacrifice. At the other end of the spectrum, the feud can be staged as a force that reduces the lovers to victims of encompassing social tensions. Such productions tend to suggest that the larger social problems represented or alluded to are intractable. Between these extremes are productions which create a more balanced tension between love and hate, in which the lovers are deeply moving and the feud is something that can be brought to an end by an older generation shocked by the destruction of their society's future. Inventing new realizations of this inherent tension is a challenge that will continue to motivate directors to stage, actors to perform, and audiences to witness this provocative tragedy – and will provide another motive for readers to conduct the mental rehearsals that are one of the rewards of reading Shakespeare's plays.

Further Reading

This guide gives details for all the books, essays, and reviews quoted in this Handbook. Many of these items will be available in both public and university libraries – as will much other material you can have the pleasure of discovering on your own. If you are just beginning to read, explore, discuss, and write about *Romeo and Juliet*, the items marked with an asterisk (*) will provide pathways for a long engagement with this play about a brief marriage.

Modern editions

* Callaghan, Dympna (ed.), *Romeo and Juliet: Texts and Contexts* (Boston, MA: Bedford-St. Martin's, 2003).

Erne, Lukas (ed.), *The First Quarto of Romeo and Juliet* (Cambridge: Cambridge University Press, 2007).

Evans, G. Blakemore (ed.), *The Riverside Shakespeare*, second edition (Boston, MA: Houghton, 1997).

Evans, G. Blakemore (ed.), *Romeo and Juliet* (Cambridge: Cambridge University Press, 2003).

Furness, Horace (ed.), *A New Variorum Edition of Shakespeare: Romeo and Juliet* (New York: Dover, 1961).

Gibbons, Brian (ed.), *Romeo and Juliet* (London: Methuen, 1980).

Hosley, Richard (ed.), *Romeo and Juliet* (New Haven and London: Yale University Press, 1954).

Kliman, Bernice W., and Laury Magnus (eds), *The Tragedy of Romeo and Juliet* (Newburyport, MA: Focus Publishing, 2008).

* Levenson, Jill L. (ed.), *Romeo and Juliet* (Oxford and New York: Oxford University Press, 2000).

Levenson, Jill L., and Barry Gaines (eds), *Romeo and Juliet, 1597*. The Malone Society Reprints (Clarendon: Oxford University Press, 2000).

* Loehlin, James N. (ed.), *Romeo and Juliet: Shakespeare in Production* (Cambridge: Cambridge University Press, 2002).

Mowat, Barbara and Paul Werstine (eds), *Romeo and Juliet* (New York: Washington Square Press, 1992).

Spencer, T.J.B. (ed.), *Romeo and Juliet* (Harmondsworth, England: Penguin, 1967).

Williams, George Walton (ed.), *The Most Excellent and Lamentable Tragedie of Romeo and Juliet* (Durham, NC: Duke University Press, 1964).

Wilson, J. Dover and G.I. Duthie (eds), *Romeo and Juliet* (Cambridge: Cambridge University Press, 1955).

The play's sources and related material

* Bullough, Geoffrey (ed.), *Narrative and Dramatic Sources of Shakespeare*, vol I: *Early Comedies, Poems, Romeo and Juliet* (London: Routledge, 1957).

Carey, John (ed.), *John Donne* (Oxford and New York: Oxford University Press, 1990).

Kuriyama, Constance Brown, *Christopher Marlowe: A Renaissance Life* (Ithaca and London: Cornell University Press, 2002).

Maclean, Hugh (ed.), *Edmund Spenser's Poetry*, second edition (New York and London: W.W. Norton, 1982).

Muir, Kenneth, *The Sources of Shakespeare's Plays* (New Haven: Yale University Press, 1978).

Prunster, Nicole (ed.), *Romeo and Juliet before Shakespeare: Early Stories of Star-Crossed Love* (Toronto: Centre of Reformation & Renaissance Studies, 2000).

Segar, Sir William, *The Book of Honor and Armes (1590) and Honor Military and Civil (1602)*, ed. Diane Bornstein (Delmar, NY: Scholar's Facsimiles and Reprints, 1975).

Spevack, Marvin (ed.), *A Complete Concordance to the Works of Shakespeare, vol. 3 Tragedies* (Hildesham: Georg Olms, 1968).

Critical studies

General studies

Blayney, Peter W.M., 'The Publication of Playbooks', in *A New History of Early English Drama*, ed. John D. Cox and David Scott Kastan (New York: Columbia University Press, 1997), pp. 383–422.

Bradley, A.C., *Shakespearean Tragedy*, fourth edition (Houndsmill, Basingstoke, Hampshire, UK: Palgrave Macmillan, 2007).

Charlton, H.B., *Shakespearian Tragedy* (Cambridge: Cambridge University Press, 1948, 1971).

Clemen, Wolfgang, *Shakespeare's Soliloquies* (London and New York: Methuen, 1987).

* Cook, Ann Jennalie, *Making a Match: Courtship in Shakespeare and His Society* (Princeton, NJ: Princeton University Press, 1991).

Dawson, Anthony B., *Watching Shakespeare: A Playgoer's Guide* (Basingstoke and London: Macmillan, 1988).

Dickey, Franklin M., *Not Wisely But Too Well: Shakespeare's Love Tragedies* (San Marino, California: The Huntington Library, 1957), pp. 63–117.

* Edelman, Charles, *Brawl Ridiculous: Swordfighting in Shakespeare's Plays* (Manchester and New York: Manchester University Press, 1992).

Evans, Bertrand, *Shakespeare's Tragic Practice* (Oxford: Clarendon Press, 1979), pp. 22–51.

Goddard, Harold, *The Meaning of Shakespeare*, vol. 1 (Chicago: University of Chicago Press, 1951), pp. 117–39.

Halliday, F.E., *The Poetry of Shakespeare's Plays* (New York: Barnes and Noble, 1964).

Hibbard, G.R., 'Love, Marriage, and Money in Shakespeare's Theatre and Shakespeare's England', in *The Elizabethan Theatre VI*, ed. George Hibbard (Hampden, CT: Archon, 1977), pp. 134–55.

Hibbard, G.R., *The Making of Shakespeare's Dramatic Poetry* (Toronto: University of Toronto Press, 1981).

Honigmann, E.A.J., *The Stability of Shakespeare's Text* (London: Edward Arnold, 1965).

Irace, Kathleen O., *Reforming the 'Bad' Quartos: Performance and Provenance of Six Shakespearean First Editions* (Newark, DE: University of Delaware Press, 1994).

Johnson, Samuel, *Johnson on Shakespeare*, in *The Yale Edition of the Works of Samuel Johnson*, vols. VII–VIII, ed. Arthur Sherbo (New Haven: Yale University Press, 1968).

Kahn, Coppélia, *Man's Estate: Masculine Identity in Shakespeare* (Berkeley, CA: University of California Press, 1981).

Kidnie, Margaret Jane, *The Shakespeare Handbooks: The Taming of the Shrew* (Houndsmill, Basingstoke, Hampshire: Palgrave Macmillan, 2006).

Slater, Ann Pasternak, *Shakespeare the Director* (Sussex, UK: Harvester Press, 1982).

Snyder, Susan, *The Comic Matrix of Shakespeare's Tragedies* (Princeton, NJ: Princeton University Press, 1979).

Stauffer, Donald A., *Shakespeare's World of Images: The Development of His Moral Ideas* (New York: Norton, 1949), pp. 53–9.

Werstine, Paul, 'Narratives About Printed Shakespeare Texts: "Foul Papers"' and "Bad" Quartos', *Shakespeare Quarterly* 41 (1990): 65–86.

Werstine, Paul, 'A Century of "Bad" Shakespeare Quartos', *Shakespeare Quarterly* 50 (1999): 310–33.

Studies of Romeo and Juliet

Dalsimer, Katherine. 'Middle Adolescence: *Romeo and Juliet*', *Female Adolescence: Psychoanalytic Reflections on Literature* (New Haven and London: Yale University Press, 1986), pp. 77–112.

Evans, Robert O., *The Osier Cage: Rhetorical Devices in Romeo and Juliet* (Lexington, KY: University of Kentucky Press, 1966).

Halio, Jay L. (ed.), *Shakespeare's Romeo and Juliet: Texts, Contexts, and Interpretation* (Newark, DE: University of Delaware Press, 1995).

Halio, Jay L. *Romeo and Juliet: A Guide to the Play* (Westport, CT and London: Greenwood Press, 1998).

* Holding, Peter, *Romeo and Juliet: Text and Performance* (Basingstoke and London: Macmillan, 1992).

Hosley, Richard, 'How Many Children Had Lady Capulet?', *Shakespeare Quarterly* 18 (1967): 3–6.

Hunter, G.K., 'Shakespeare Earliest Tragedies: *Titus Andronicus* and *Romeo and Juliet*', *Shakespeare Survey* 27 (1974): 1–9.

Lawlor, John, '*Romeo and Juliet*', in *Early Shakespeare*, ed. John Russell Brown and B. Harris (London: Edward Arnold, 1961), pp. 123–43.

McCown, Gary, '"Runnawayes' Eyes" and Juliet's Epithalamium', *Shakespeare Quarterly* 27 (1976): 150–70.

Porter, Joseph A., *Shakespeare's Mercutio: His History and Drama* (Chapel Hill, NC, and London: University of North Carolina Press, 1988).

* Roberts, Sasha, *William Shakespeare's Romeo and Juliet* (Plymouth, UK: Northcote House, 1998).

Snyder, Susan, 'Ideology and Feud in *Romeo and Juliet*', *Shakespeare Survey* 49 (1996): 87–96.

Urkowitz, Steven, 'Good News About "Bad" Quartos', in *'Bad' Shakespeare: Revaluations of the Shakespeare Canon*, ed. Maurice Charney (Rutherford, Madison, Teaneck, NJ: Fairleigh Dickinson University Press, 1988), pp. 189–206.

Urkowitz, Steven, '*Romeo and Juliet* and the Socialization of Dramatic Characters' (Unpublished manuscript, 2008).

* Watts, Cedric, *Romeo and Juliet* (Boston, MA: G.K. Hall, 1991).

Performance and theater studies

General studies

Allam, Roger, 'Mercutio in *Romeo and Juliet*', in *Players of Shakespeare 2*, ed. Russell Jackson and Robert Smallwood (Cambridge: Cambridge University Press, 1988), pp. 107–19.

* Brown, John Russell, *Discovering Shakespeare: A Guide to the Plays* (New York: Columbia University Press, 1981).

* Dessen, Alan C., '*Romeo opens the tomb*', in *Recovering Shakespeare's Theatrical Vocabulary* (Cambridge: Cambridge University Press, 1995), pp. 176–95.

Dessen, Alan C., 'Rescripting History and the Supernatural: Shakespeare on the Stage in 2000', *Shakespeare Bulletin* 19 (Winter, 2001): 5–9.

Goldman, Michael, '*Romeo and Juliet*: The Meaning of a Theatrical Experience', in *Shakespeare and the Energies of Drama* (Princeton, NJ: Princeton University Press, 1972), pp. 33–44.

* Granville-Barker, Harley, *Prefaces to Shakespeare II* (Princeton, NJ: Princeton University Press, 1947).

* Gurr, Andrew, 'The Date and Expected Venue of *Romeo and Juliet*', *Shakespeare Survey* 49 (1996): 15–25.

Hogan, Charles B., *Shakespeare in the Theatre, 1701–1800*, 2 vols. (Oxford: Oxford University Press, 1952).

Hosley, Richard, 'The Discovery Space in Shakespeare's Globe', *Shakespeare Survey* 12 (1959): 35–46.

* Jackson, Russell, *Romeo and Juliet* (Birmingham: Arden, 2002).

Kennedy, Dennis, *Looking at Shakespeare: A Visual History of Twentieth Century Performance* (Cambridge: Cambridge University Press, 1993).

*Levenson, Jill. *Shakespeare in Performance: Romeo and Juliet* (Manchester: Manchester University Press, 1987).

Lower, Charles B., '*Romeo and Juliet*, IV.v: A Stage Direction and Purposeful Comedy', *Shakespeare Studies* 8 (1975): 177–94.

O'Connor, John and Katharine Goodland (eds), *A Directory of Shakespeare in Performance 1970–2005: Volume 1: Great Britain* (Basingstoke: Palgrave Macmillan, 2007).

Sprague, Arthur Colby, *Shakespeare and the Actors: The Stage Business of His Plays 1660–1905* (New York: Russell and Russell, 1963).

Tennant, David, 'Romeo in *Romeo and Juliet*', in *Players of Shakespeare 5*, ed. Robert Smallwood (Cambridge: Cambridge University Press, 2003), pp. 113–30.

Thomson, Leslie, ' "With patient ears attend": *Romeo and Juliet* on the Elizabethan Stage', *Studies in Philology*, 92 (1995): 230–47.

Trewin, J.C., *Shakespeare on the English Stage 1900–1964* (London: Barrie and Rockliff, 1964).

* Wright, Katherine L., *Shakespeare's Romeo and Juliet in Performance: Traditions and Departures* (Lewiston, Queenston, Lampeter: Edwin Mellen Press, 1997).

Garrick and other early productions

Branam, George C., 'The Genesis of David Garrick's *Romeo and Juliet*', *Shakespeare Quarterly* 35 (1984): 170–9.

Burnim, Kalman A., *David Garrick, Director* (Carbondale and Edwardsville, IL: Southern Illinois University Press, 1973).

Downes, John, *Roscius Anglicanus* (1708), The Augustan Reprint Society, Publication #134 (Los Angeles, CA: William Andrews Clark Memorial Library, 1969).

Garrick, David, *The Plays of David Garrick, Volume 3: Garrick's Adaptations of Shakespeare*, ed. Harry William Pedicord and Frederick Louis

Bergmann (Carbondale and Edwardsville, IL: Southern Illinois University Press, 1981), pp. 76–149.

Garrick, David, *Romeo and Juliet* (1750). Cornmarket Press Facsimile from the copy in Birmingham Shakespeare Library (London: Cornmarket Press, 1969).

Gielgud

Ashcroft, Peggy, 'Playing Shakespeare', *Shakespeare Survey* 40 (1987): 11–19.

Barker, Felix, *The Oliviers: A Biography* (London: Hamish Hamilton, 1953).

Burton, Hal (ed.), *Great Acting* (New York: Hill and Wang, 1967).

Cookman, A.V., *The New York Times*, 17 November 1935.

Farjeon, Herbert, *The Shakespearean Scene: Dramatic Criticism* (London: Hutchinson, 1949).

Gielgud, John, with John Miller, *Acting Shakespeare* (New York: Scribner's 1991).

West Side Story

Beckerman, Bernard and Howard Siegman (eds), *On Stage: Selected Theater Reviews from The New York Times 1920–1970* (New York: Arno, 1973).

Houghton, Norris, 'Introduction', *Romeo and Juliet/West Side Story* (New York: Dell, 1965), pp. 7–14.

Laurents, Arthur, *Mainly on Directing: Gypsy, West Side Story, and Other Musicals* (New York: Alfred A. Knopf, 2009).

Secrest, Meryle, *Stephen Sondheim: A Life* (New York: Alfred A. Knopf, 1998).

Bogdanov

Berkowitz, Gerald M., 'Shakespeare in London, January-July 1987', *Shakespeare Quarterly* 38 (1987): 495–500.

Billington, Michael, *One Night Stands: A Critic's View of Modern British Theatre* (London: Nick Hearn Books, 1993).

Bogdanov, Michael, *Shakespeare – The Director's Cut: Essays on Shakespeare's Plays*, vol. 1 (Edinburgh, Capercaillie Books, 2003).

Bruce, Brenda, 'Nurse in *Romeo and Juliet*', in *Players of Shakespeare*, ed. Philip Brockbank (Cambridge: Cambridge University Press, 1985), pp. 91–101.

Cusack, Niamh, 'Juliet in *Romeo and Juliet*', in *Players of Shakespeare 2*, ed. Russell Jackson and Robert Smallwood (Cambridge: Cambridge University Press, 1988), pp. 121–35.

Dessen, Alan C., 'What's New? Shakespeare on Stage in 1986', *Shakespeare Quarterly* 38 (1987): 90–6.

Shrimpton, Nicholas, 'Shakespeare Performances in London, Manchester, and Stratford-upon-Avon 1985–6', *Shakespeare Survey* 40 (1987): 178–80.

Warren, Roger, 'Shakespeare at Stratford-upon-Avon, 1986', *Shakespeare Quarterly* 38 (1987): 82–9.

Paparelli

Benton, Nicholas F., 'Folger's "Romeo & Juliet" Reveals Consequences of Parental Abuse', *Falls Church News-Press*, 20 January 2005.

Graham, Trey, 'Will and Grace', *Washington City Paper*, 21 January 2005.

Ponick, T.L., *The Washington Times*, 21 January 2005.

Film, television, and audio productions

Romeo and Juliet (1936), dir. George Cukor. 125 minutes. B & W. DVD.

Romeo and Juliet (1954), dir. Renato Castellani. 138 minutes, Color (Technicolor). VHS.

Romeo and Juliet (1968), dir. Franco Zefirreli. 138 minutes, Color (Technicolor). DVD.

Romeo and Juliet (1978), dir. Alvin Rakoff. BBC-Time/Life. DVD.

Romeo + Juliet (1996), dir. Baz Luhrmann. 120 minutes. Color (Deluxe). DVD.

West Side Story (1961), dir. Jerome Robbins and Robert Wise. 152 minutes. Color (Technicolor). DVD.

Historical Shakespeare Recordings by Henry Irving, Ellen Terry, and others. CD release 2000.

Romeo and Juliet (1961), dir. Howard Sackler. With Claire Bloom and Albert Finney. Audiocasette release 1990.

Romeo and Juliet, dir. Kenneth Branagh and Glyn Dearman. With Samantha Bond and Kenneth Branagh. CD release 1993.

Romeo and Juliet, dir. Michael Sheen. With Kate Beckinsale and Michael Sheen. CD release 1997.

Romeo and Juliet, dir. Clive Brill. With Maria Miles and Joseph Fiennes. CD release 2003.

Film and television studies

Brown, John Russell, 'Zeffirelli's *Romeo and Juliet*', in *Shakespeare's Plays in Performance* (Harmondsworth, England: Penguin, 1969), pp. 181–93.

* Buhler, Stephen M., *Shakespeare in the Cinema: Ocular Proof* (Albany, NY: State University of New York Press, 2002).

* Cartmell, Deborah, *Interpreting Shakespeare on Screen* (New York: St. Martin's Press, 2000).

* Crowl, Samuel, *Shakespeare and Film: A Norton Guide* (New York and London: Norton, 2008).

Dench, Judi, 'A Career in Shakespeare', in *Shakespeare: An Illustrated Stage History*, ed. Jonathan Bate and Russell Jackson (Oxford: Oxford University Press, 1996), pp. 197–210.

* Jorgens, Jack, *Shakespeare on Film* (Bloomington and London: Indiana University Press, 1977).

Loehlin, James N., ' "These Violent Delights Have Violent Ends": Baz Luhrmann's Millenial Shakespeare', in *Shakespeare, Film, Fin de Siècle*, ed. Mark Thornton Burnett and Ramona Wray (Basingstoke: Macmillan Press, 2000).

Pearce, Craig, and Baz Luhrmann, *William Shakespeare's 'Romeo + Juliet'* (New York: Bantam Doubleday Dell, 1996).

* Rothwell, Kenneth S., *A History of Shakespeare on Screen: A Century of Film and Television* (Cambridge: Cambridge University Press, 1999).

Tatspaugh, Patricia, 'The Tragedies of Love on Film', in *The Cambridge Companion to Shakespeare on Film*, ed. Russell Jackson (Cambridge: Cambridge University Press, 2000), pp. 135–43.

Tynan, Kenneth, *Tynan Right and Left: Plays, Films, People, Places and Events* (New York: Atheneum, 1967).

Willson, Jr., Robert F. 'Star-Crossed Generations: Three Film Versions of *Romeo and Juliet*', in *Approaches to Teaching Shakespeare's Romeo and Juliet*, ed. Maurice Hunt (New York: MLA, 2000), pp. 179–85.

Zeffirelli, Franco, *Directors on Directing: A Sourcebook of the Modern Theater*, ed. Toby Cole and Helen Krich Chinoy (Indianapolis, IN: Bobbs-Merrill, 1976).

Zeffirelli, Franco, 'Filming Shakespeare: Franco Zeffirelli', in *Staging Shakespeare: Seminars on Production Problems*, ed. Glenn Loney (New York and London: Garland Publishing, 1990), pp. 239–70.

Index